MW01628797

To Rick and Jody ,

Life is a never-ending story

Chris P. [illegible]

Phil 4:8-9

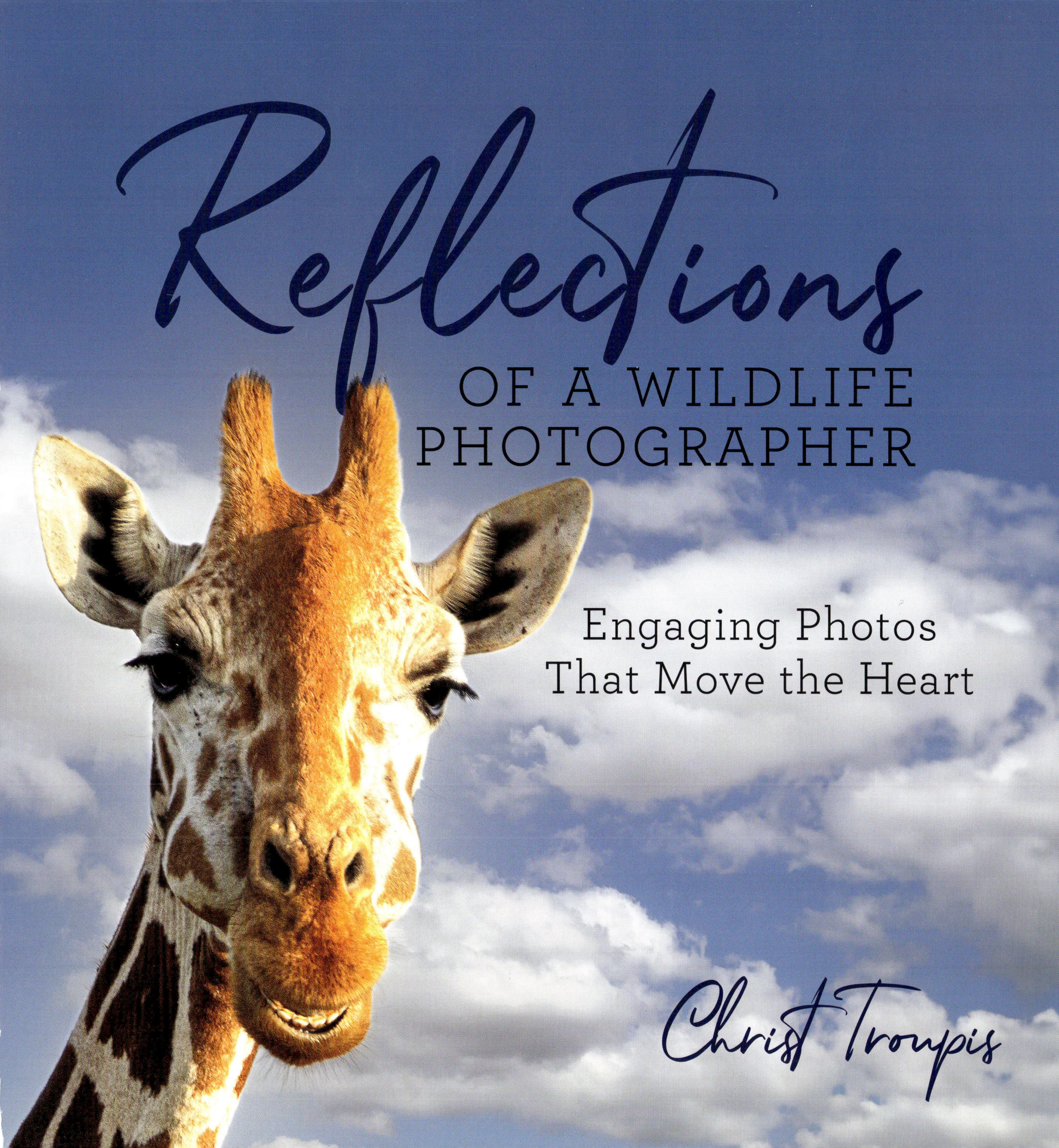
Reflections
OF A WILDLIFE
PHOTOGRAPHER
Engaging Photos
That Move the Heart
Christ Troupis

Reflections of a Wildlife Photographer
Engaging Photos That Move the Heart

Front cover: reticulated giraffe
Back cover: bald eagles

Cover & Interior Design: Aloha Publishing

Print ISBN: 978-1-61206-297-6

To learn more, visit: ChristTroupis.com

Christ Troupis PHOTOGRAPHY

Printed in Canada

This book is dedicated to two beautiful talented women, my wife, Maureen, and our daughter, Kristen, who have both encouraged and supported my love and sometimes obsession with photography and wildlife. My love of the outdoors was rekindled by Kristen's life on the road chronicled in her blog, *Bearfoot Theory,* at BearfootTheory.com. Maureen and Kristen are the loves of my life, and so it is with the greatest of affection I dedicate my art back to these two artists.

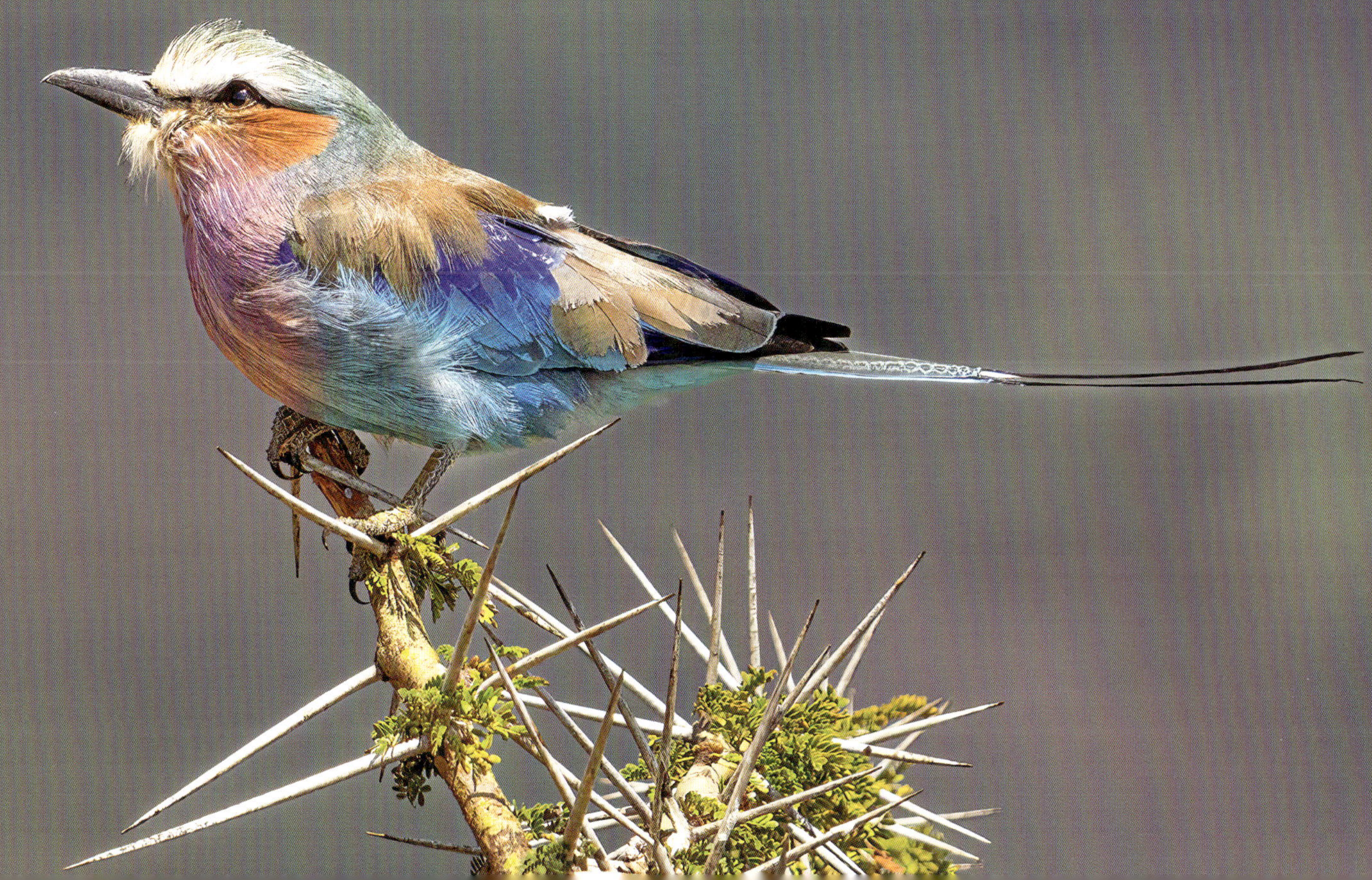

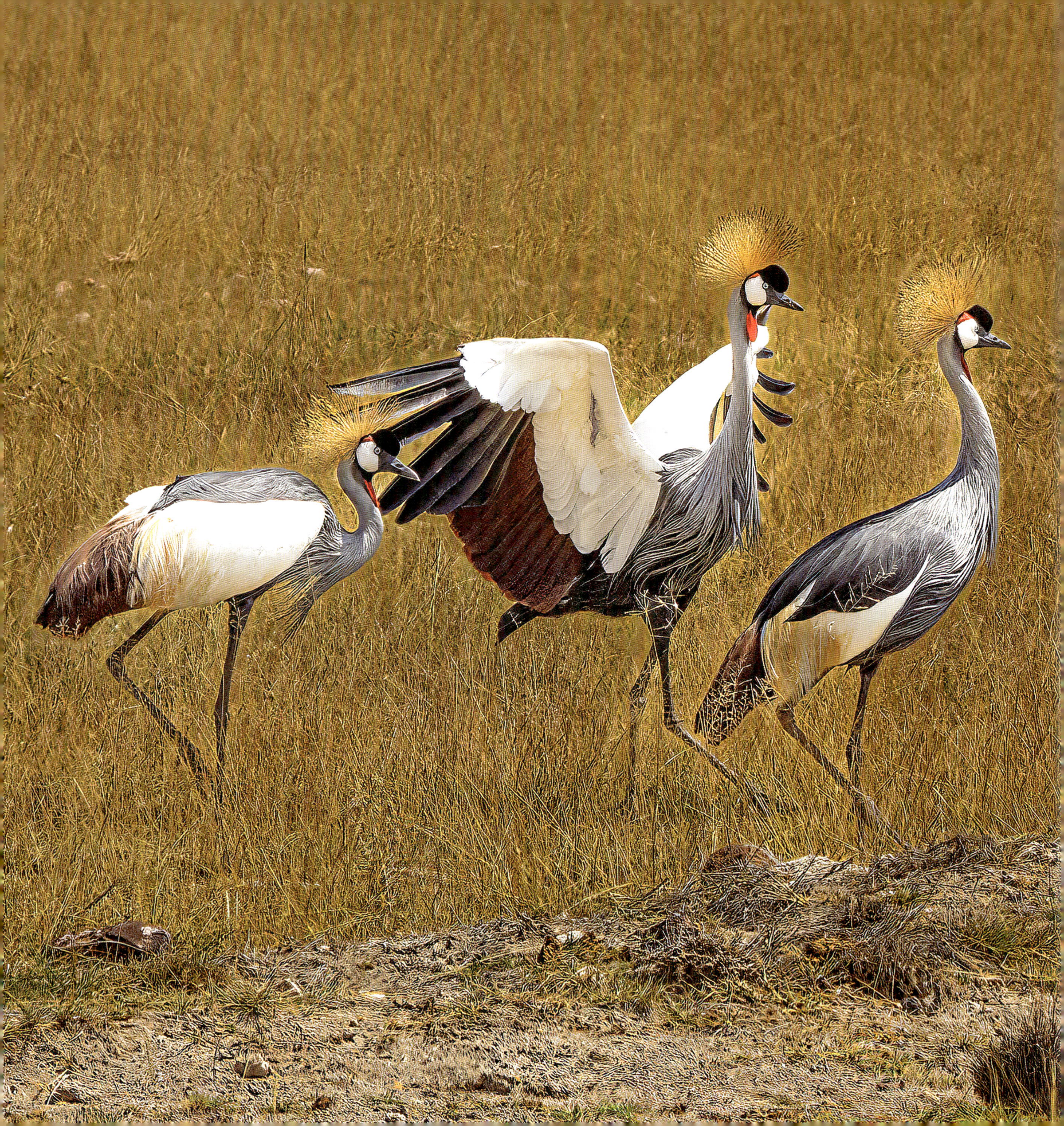

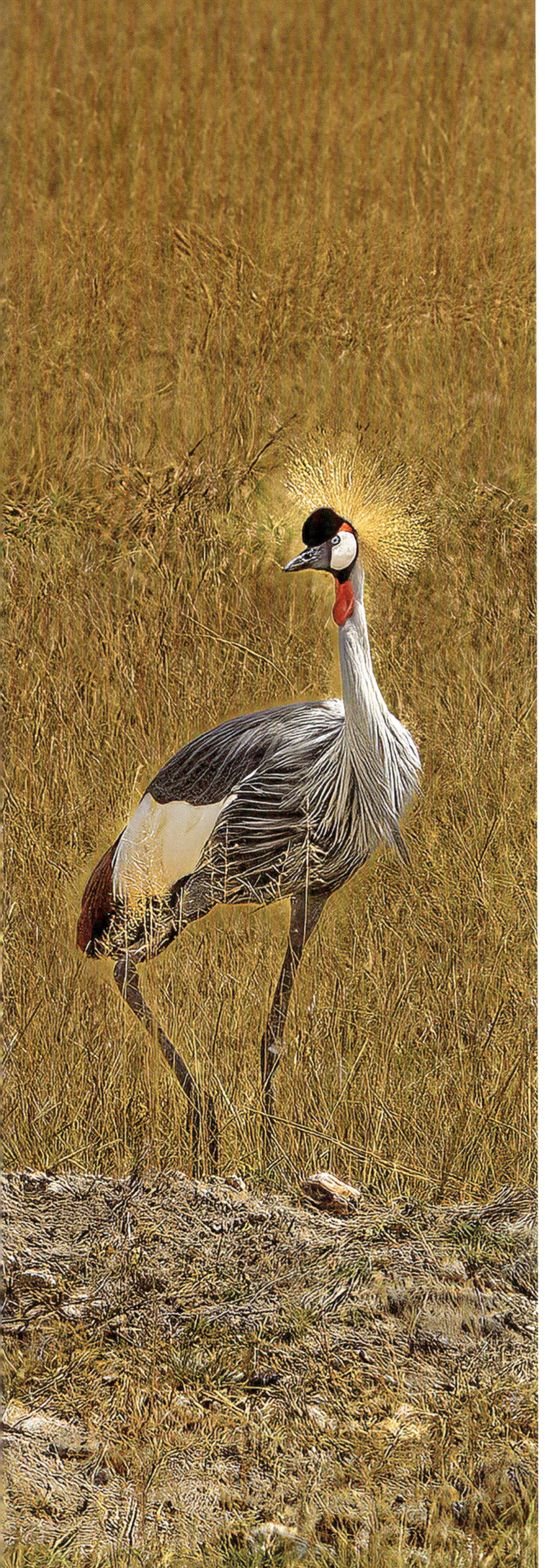

Reflections

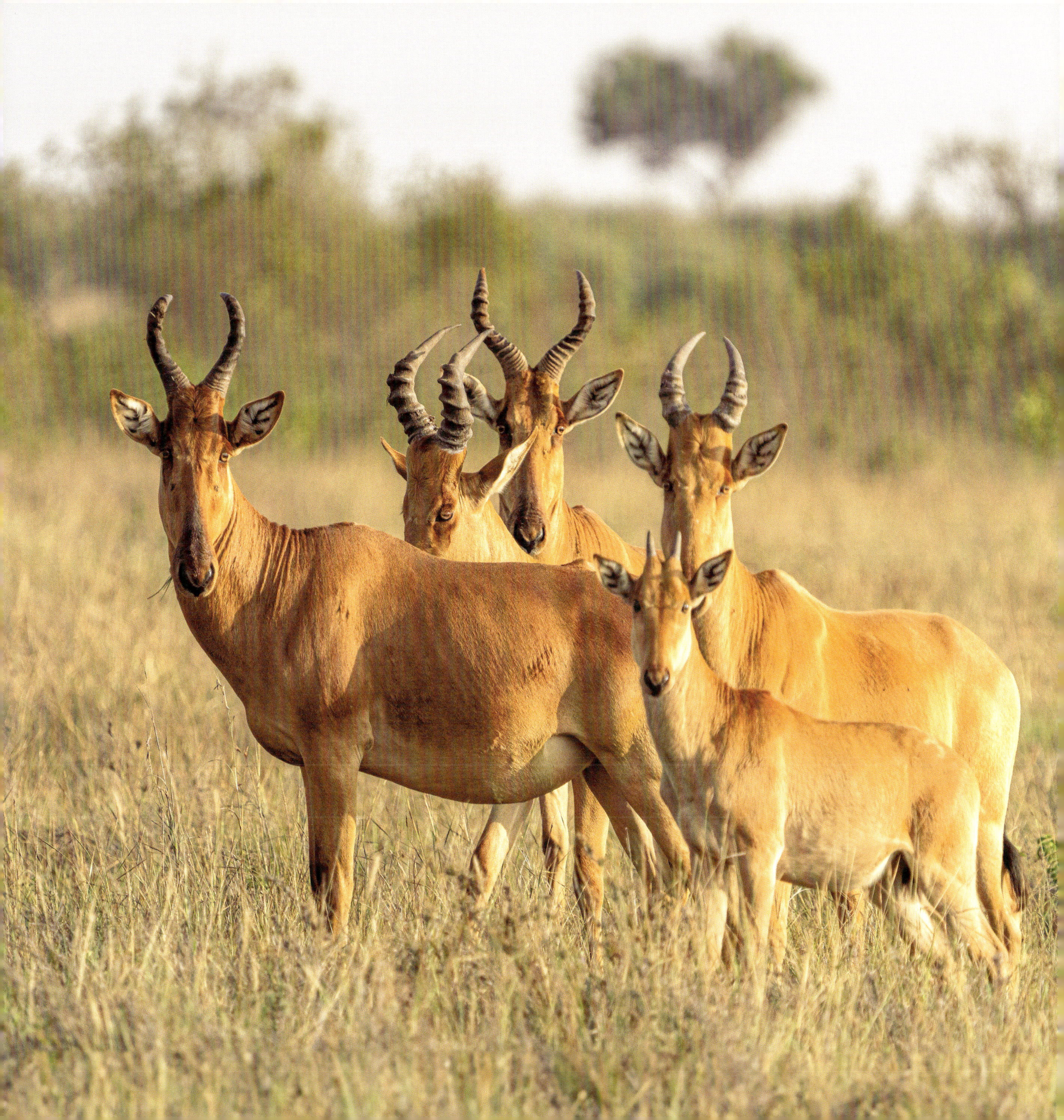

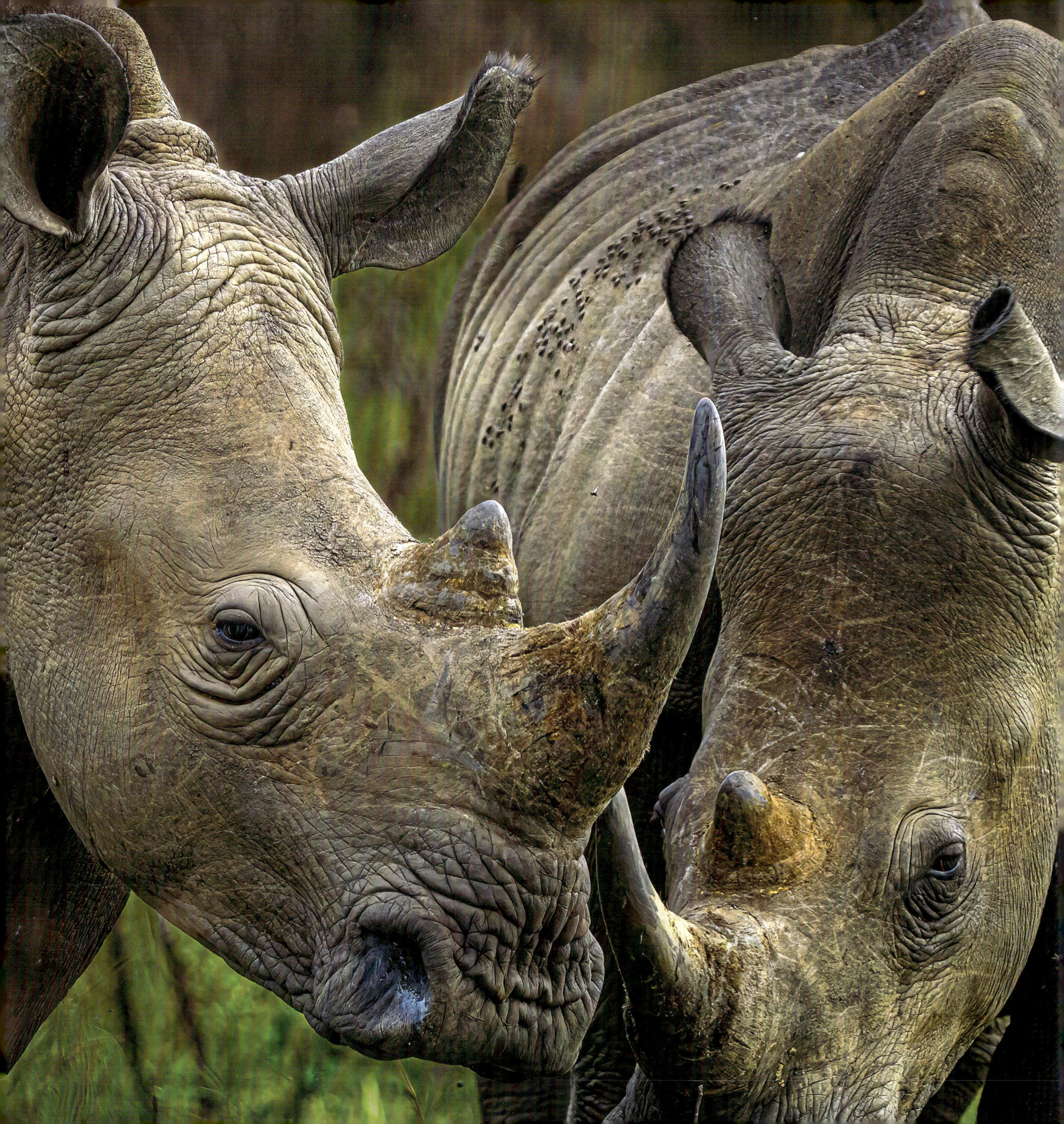

How long did it take to paint a Renaissance masterpiece? Hours and days passed while the artist labored to record minute details of a face, preserve a pose, or re-create the interaction of shadows and light. How did the artist accurately portray that one moment when he could only record it one tiny fraction at a time? Is the result a true reflection of that first look? Or do we see a composite from many days of modeling? In the end, the artist's work is entirely his own because he has to meld everything to fit his own memory of that first sitting. And memory is personal.

When you look at a painting, you see only the artist's memory of what he saw. The original image, colored by the artist's vision of it, merges and becomes something new. And that's what he wants you to see and ponder.

Photography is different. With one click of a button, we can preserve in perfect detail the exact scene. We can capture that moment in time. And for me, the greatest joy is in doing just that. Nothing compares to locking eyes with a wild bird or animal and becoming so engrossed in their lives that all other thoughts disappear.

So, when does the photo become art? When the photographer is actively involved. Then the result evokes emotion. My goal is for you to see what I saw, on and beneath the surface; for you to feel what I felt—the same emotional attachment to the subject. If my photo draws you in and makes you linger for more than a few seconds, then you have made that connection. If an image draws your attention, engages you, and relaxes your mind—even if just for a moment—the photo becomes art.

1.

The Ghost and the Darkness

The thrill of my life has been the opportunity to see and photograph the mighty beasts that still roam the African savannahs. There is something about sitting in an open vehicle just after sunrise a few feet away from a "man-eater." It gets your blood running faster than two shots of espresso.

In 1898, the British were building a railway from Mombasa on the Indian Ocean to Lake Victoria through Tanzania. But workers abandoned the project when a pair of lions began to stalk the camps, dragging people from their tents at night and eating them alive. Over a period of nine months, it was reported that the two, called the Ghost and the Darkness by natives, had killed 135 workers. The number may have been much higher since many deaths in surrounding villages went unreported. Researchers later could only definitively establish that the two had killed and eaten at least 35.

You probably know that lions are ferocious. But until you see one up close in the wild, you can't imagine the reality. On the savanna that day, I saw the food that had been laid out and knew the lions were coming. I thought I was ready. I wasn't. They came so fast it took my breath away. Over 400 pounds of teeth, claw, sinew, and muscle roaring toward you.

What an eye-opener to visit a world where you are nowhere near the top of the food chain. Everything in the wild is faster than you, and you are much easier to eat than something with hoofs and horns. By the way, *The Ghost and the Darkness* is a great film about the lions of Tsavo. I highly recommend it, but not if you are planning on tent camping in the near future.

These man-eaters were drawn in by fresh meat dropped by our guide. I was nervous and adrenaline was high as I readied my shot from a reinforced blind.

VICTORIA FALLS NP, ZIMBABWE | ISO 160 | 120MM | 1/1000

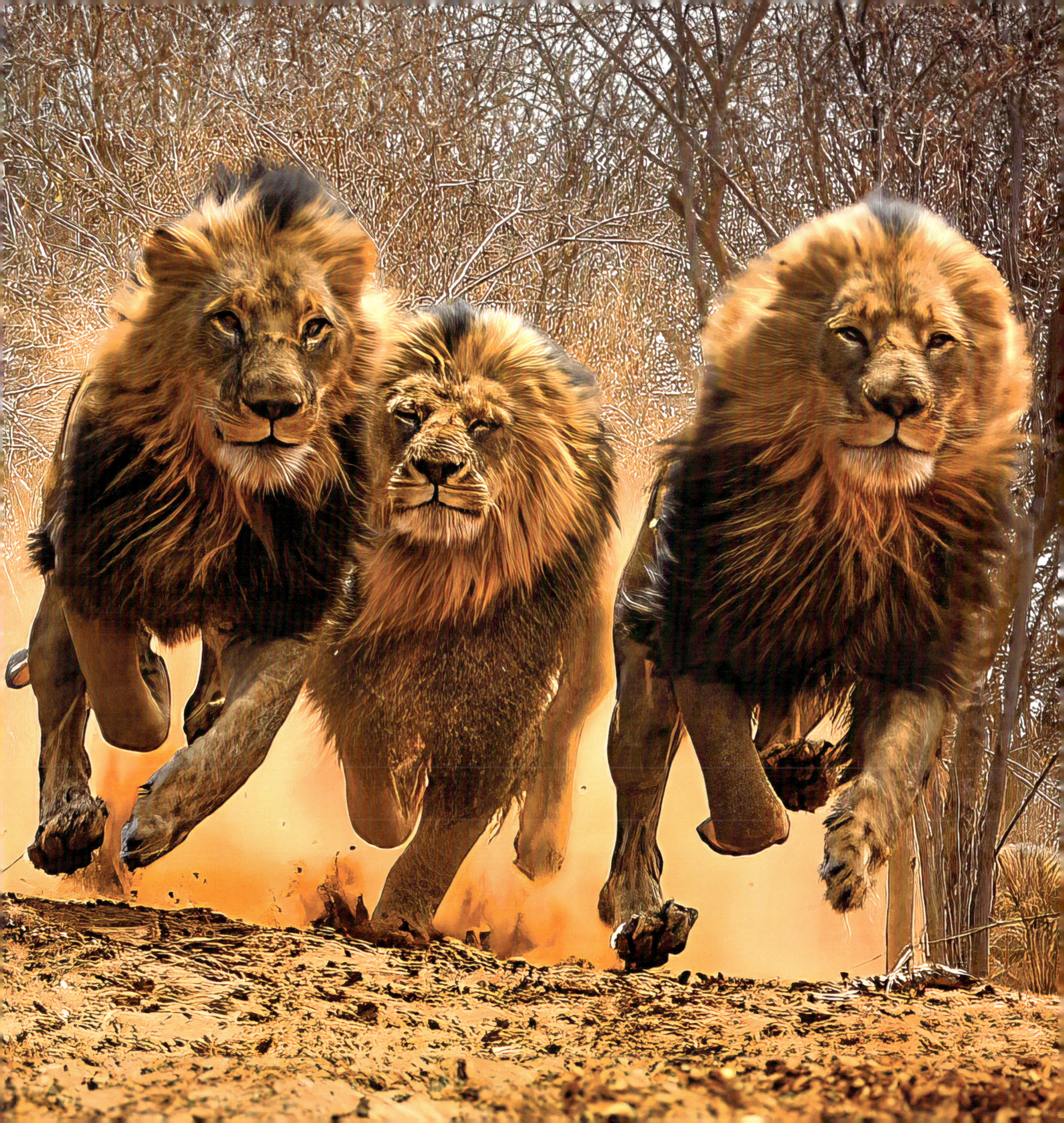

Behind that moose's engaging smile lurks a cantankerous, unpredictable, and very dangerous beastie, just waiting to stomp the living daylights out of you if you get too close.

In 2011, we lost Moses, our West Highland Terrier. He was 18 years old, practically blind, arthritic, and with all the usual ailments of age. Moses was very cute. But looks can be deceiving. He was beyond cranky and didn't seem to like anyone but me. In fact, Maureen and just about everyone else said he was downright mean. Their conclusion was amply supported by the fact that he bit just about everyone but me over his last few years. But I made excuses for him. We had an understanding. Moses was my dog. I took him to my office, and he slept under my desk while I worked. I miss him terribly.

When Moses died, my sister-in-law bought me a toy Scotty dog to cheer me up. It played Maurice Chevalier singing "Put on a Happy Face." It was a tonic for me.

I occasionally play the song. It always brings a smile to my face and a few tears, like this smiling Yellowstone moose. Don't trust him. But just look at that smile and put on a happy face.

This moose was in deep cover next to an open meadow. I crouched and waited as he eventually walked out of the brush and looked back.

YELLOWSTONE NP, WYOMING | ISO 640 | 500MM | 1/250

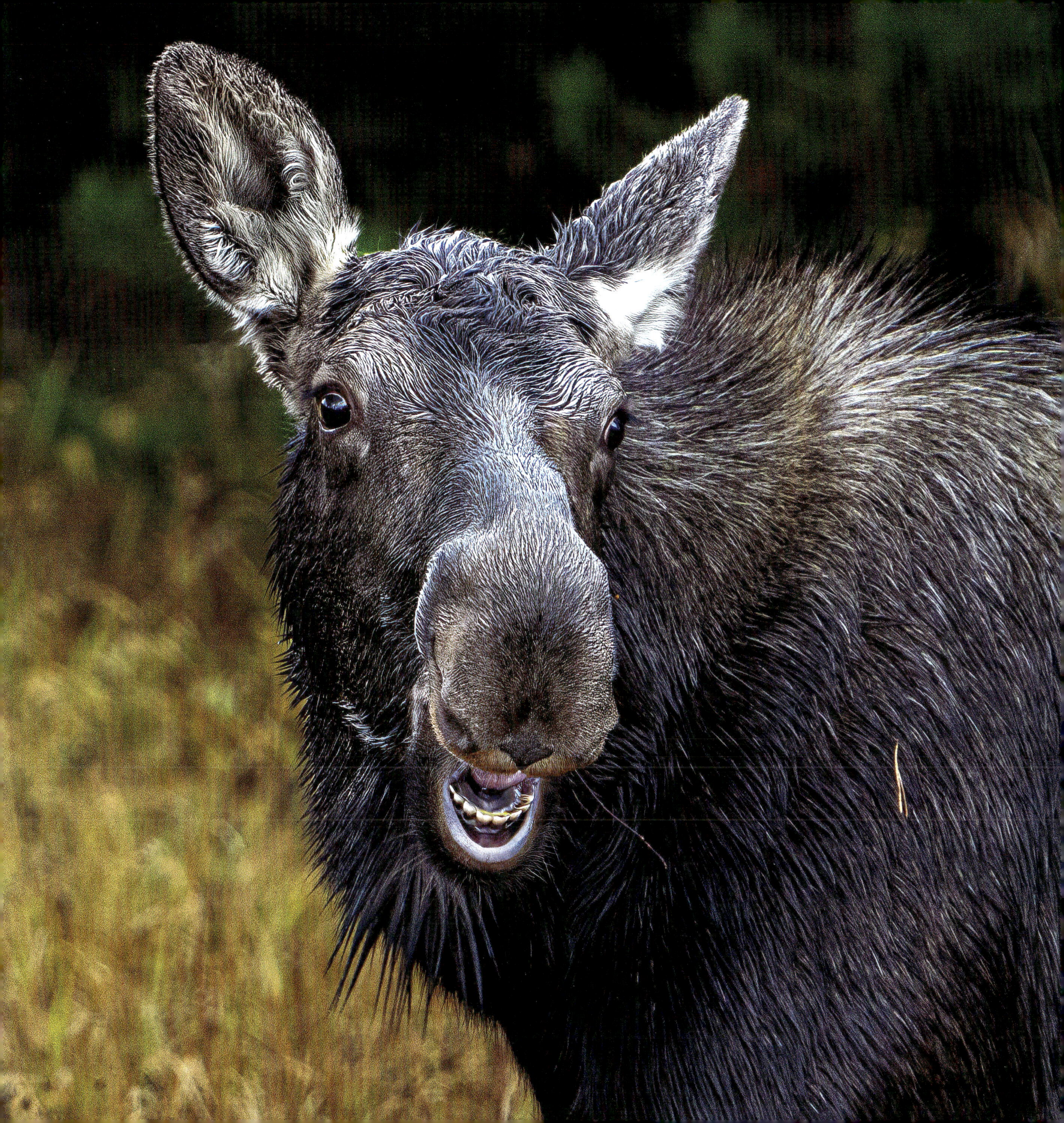

3.

Clown of the Sea

This red-footed booby is building a nest at the Kilauea Lighthouse on the island of Kauai. AllAboutBirds.org describes them this way:

"The red-footed booby is a graceful, slim-winged seabird named for its vivid coral-red feet, which males show off during courtship. Females choose males with the brightest feet. Red-footed boobies pursue fish by diving into the sea, but also chase flying fish like a flycatcher chases flies."

Because boobies don't fear humans, they often land in fishermen's boats. Unfortunately for them, Spanish fishermen are not, as a general rule, vegetarians. Because these face-painted birds with red feet were so easy to fool into the dinner pot, Spaniards named them "booby," which, in Spanish, means clown or fool.

A booby's red feet come from the fish it eats. The fish eat plants; the plants have pigments in them that also produce bright yellow, red, and orange colors in plants, vegetables, and fruits. So, the better a booby is at fishing, the more fish he eats, the more pigment he ingests, and the brighter his feet become, which in turn attracts potential mates.

The result of this natural selection process is that the strongest providers attract female mates because their feet are the brightest, which constantly improves the genetic stock of the species.

I guess you are what you eat. But given the result, it sure doesn't sound like they are "boobies" after all, does it?

I set up the shot at the nest and waited for the bird's approach, refocusing on the bird just before it landed to ensure correct focus.

KAUAI, HAWAII | ISO 1000 | 498MM | 1/3200

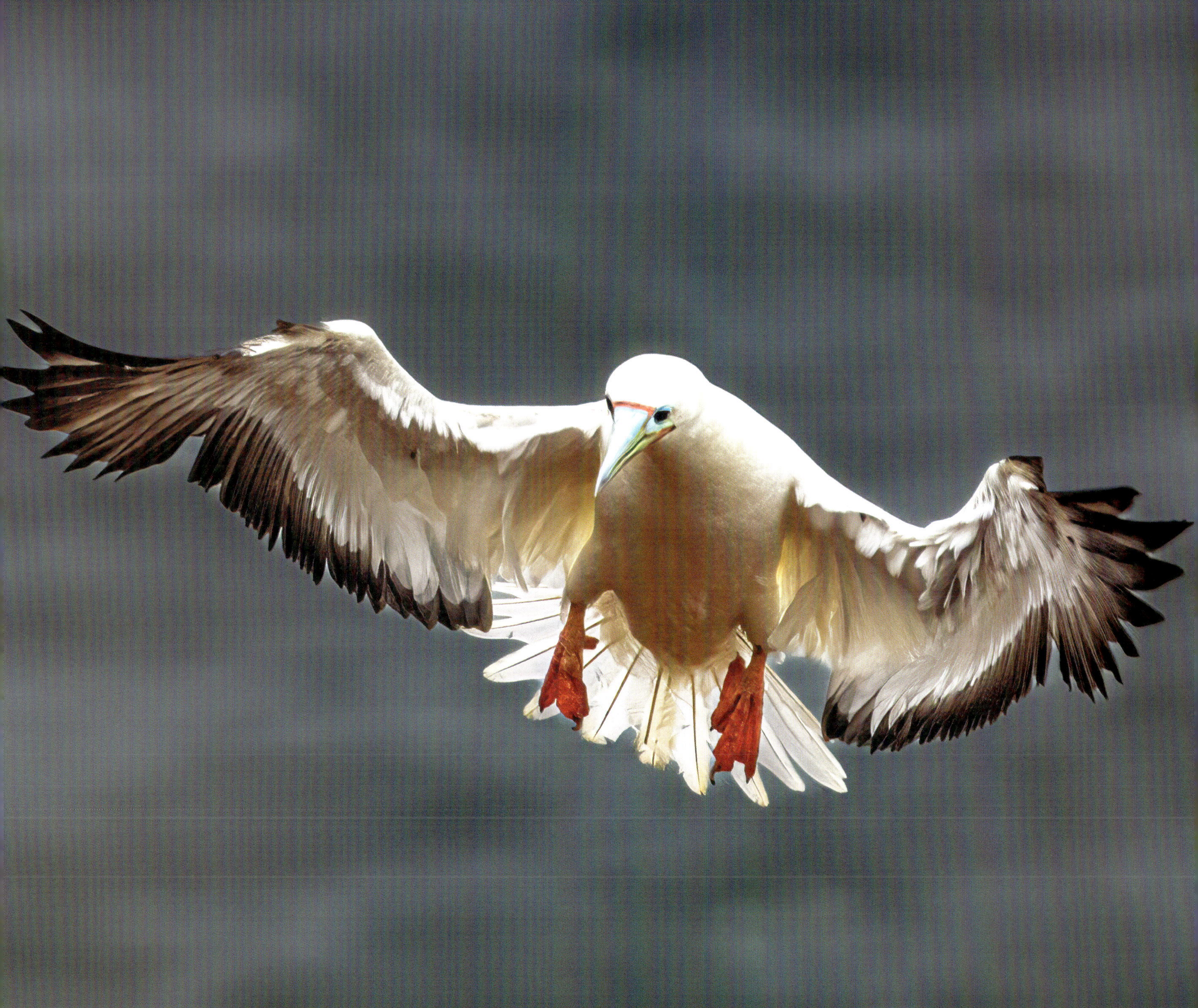

4.

Whistler's Wings

Among the most beautiful ducks to visit Idaho in winter is the Barrow's goldeneye. The male has a striking appearance with his blue head. This species comes from as far as Alaska.

Todd Peterson of BirdNote.org gives the best description of them:

> You may get to know these birds by sound as much as sight.
>
> On a still winter afternoon, walking the shore of Puget or Long Island Sound, you'll hear them coming low across the water. Goldeneyes, also known as "whistlers," their wings sibilant, make the sound, as Ernest Hemingway wrote, of ripping silk.
>
> You're likely to see their piercing golden eyes and the striking domino black-and-white of the male's plumage as you board a ferry or travel by boat along the shore.
>
> Sometimes in squadrons, they dive for crustaceans and mollusks.
>
> Autumn brings both species of goldeneyes, common and Barrow's. You'll know the male Barrow's by the half-moon of white between its brilliant yellow eye and short bill.
>
> Enjoy them now while you can. In spring, goldeneyes will be gone, returning to the boreal forests of Canada and Alaska to breed and hatch their young in the cavities of trees. And you'll have to wait until next November to hear again the music of their wings.

Waiting at the river's edge, I watched the ducks that were moving slowly in the current come closer to me and choose a wide-open aperture to blur the rocks in the background.

EAGLE ISLAND SP, IDAHO | ISO 1600 | 840MM | 1/1000

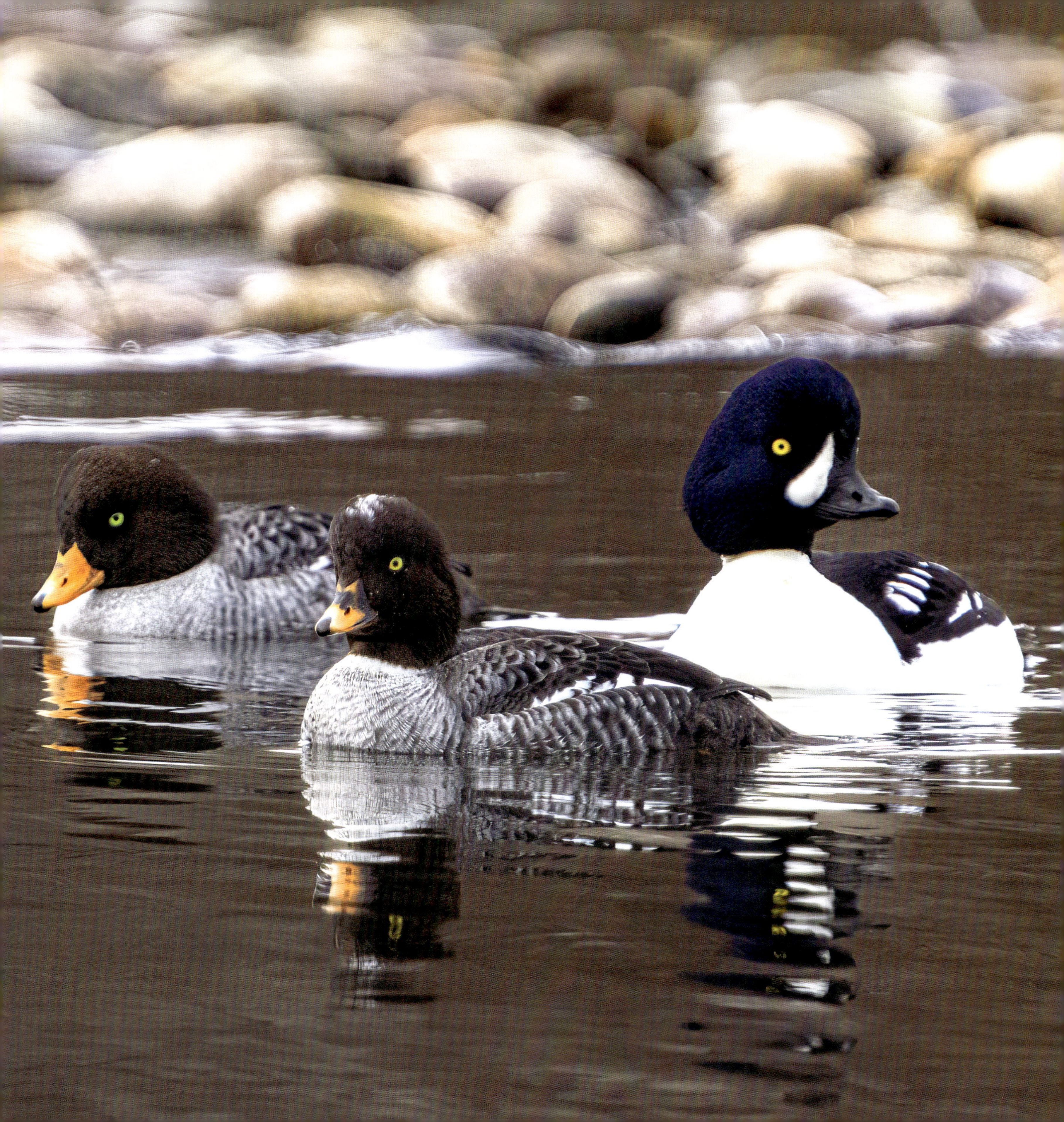

5.

Alone

This 4-year-old male grizzly cub is trying to catch a salmon. It is his first time without his mother's help. She booted him out because she was about to have a new cub to raise. For a male grizzly, he is in his awkward "tweens."

The plaintive forlorn look in his eyes and his gaunt features tell you his whole story. On his own at four, he has to feed and defend himself now and for the rest of his life, which he will live alone. Male grizzly bears live a solitary life except during a brief mating season. What a sad way to live!

When I think of his plight, I am so grateful for friends and family who have filled my life with love and joy. Above all, I am thankful that God loves me and calls me His child because, with Him, I am never alone. (John 1:12)

Solomon, the wise king, wrote:

"Two people are better off than one, for they can help each other succeed. If one person falls, the other can reach out and help. But someone who falls alone is in real trouble." Ecclesiastes 4:9-10 (NLT)

In the final analysis, loving relationships are the only things that have eternal value.

I leaned down to the water level to take this shot from a boat 10 feet away so I could be at this grizzly cub's eye level.

KODIAK ISLAND, ALASKA | ISO 640 | 200MM | 1/500

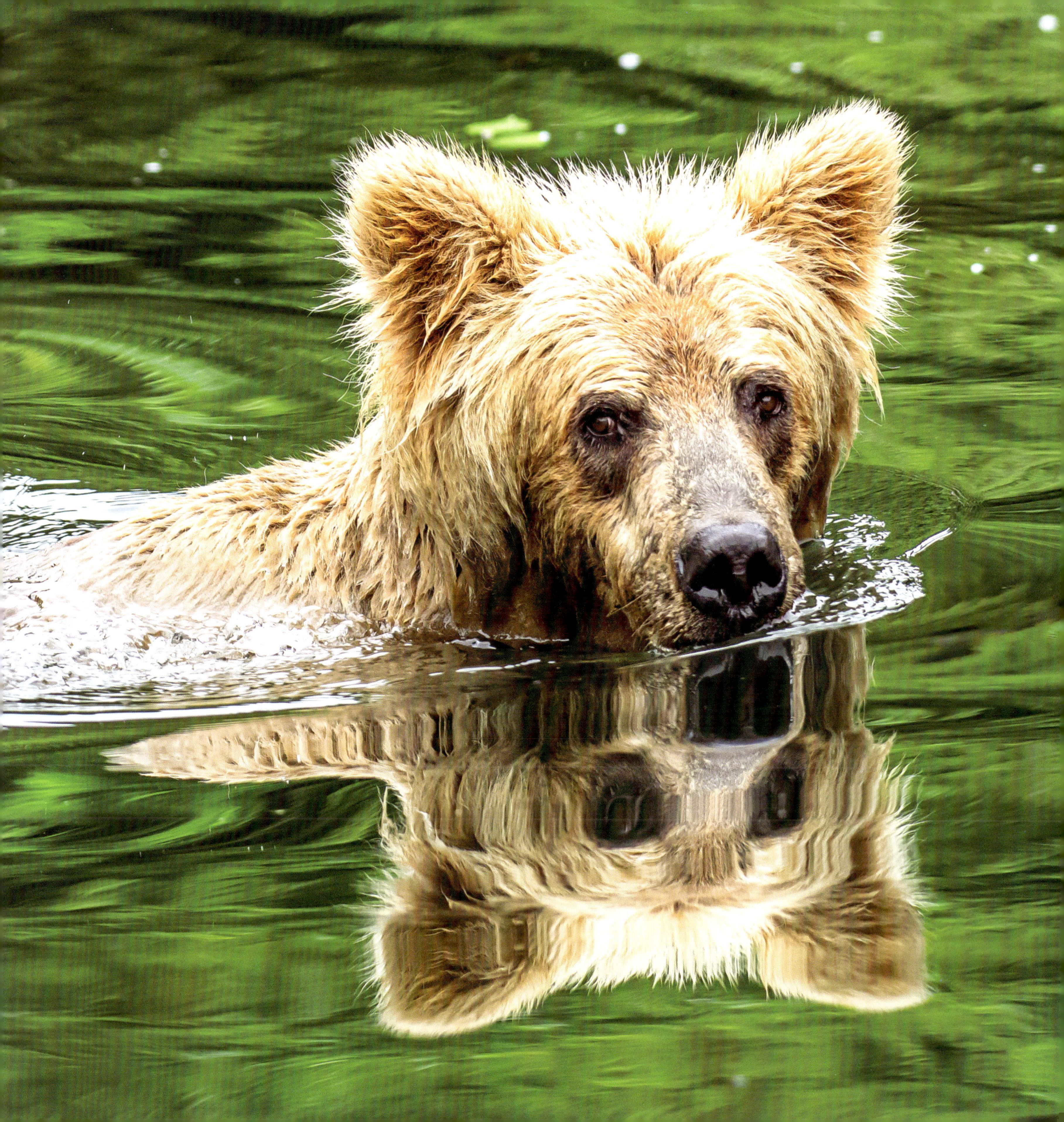

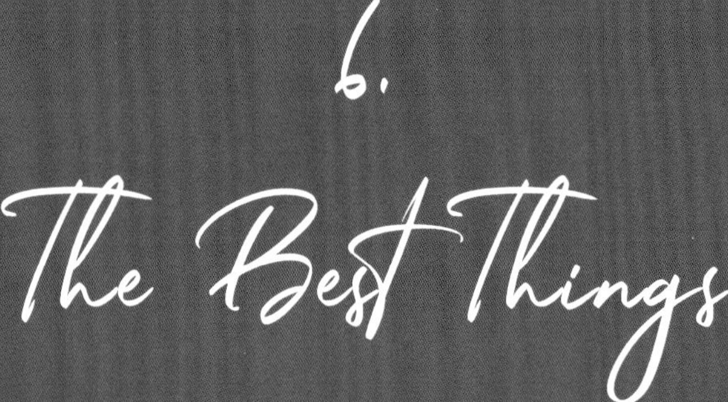

6. The Best Things

Valentine's Day is here. I hope you have made plans to celebrate that special someone in your life. After more than 37 wonderful years together, Maureen still gets my heart racing. I am sure that many of you feel the same about your significant other.

I deeply love my wife. However, as a man, I sometimes struggle with how to express that love. A few days ago, we decided to take a leisurely walk on the Boise River Greenbelt. Thinking it was just a casual stroll, I left my camera behind.

As we strolled down the riverbank, I found myself completely engrossed by the vibrant ducks, an elegant heron soaring above, and a Cooper's hawk nestled in a nearby thicket. But I didn't consider my wandering eye to be an act of infidelity. After all, these were birds, not "chicks."

But while I was lost in this natural spectacle, unbeknownst to me, Maureen began to mimic the birds' movements, flapping her arms in a comedic manner reminiscent of the chicken dance we often see at weddings. When I finally noticed and gave her a puzzled look, she exclaimed, "It seems I need to act like a bird to catch your eye!"

A few weeks later, our pastor made this very important observation: "Sometimes we are so busy doing good things that we don't have time left for the best things." I love photography. But it is just one of the good things. Maureen is and will always be the best thing in my life. I cherish her deeply. And I vow to spend the remainder of our days ensuring she never feels the need to perform a bird dance to secure my attention or love.

The sun was setting and the water's reflection in the fading light created this soft exposure.

EAGLE, IDAHO | ISO 160 | 840MM | 1/250

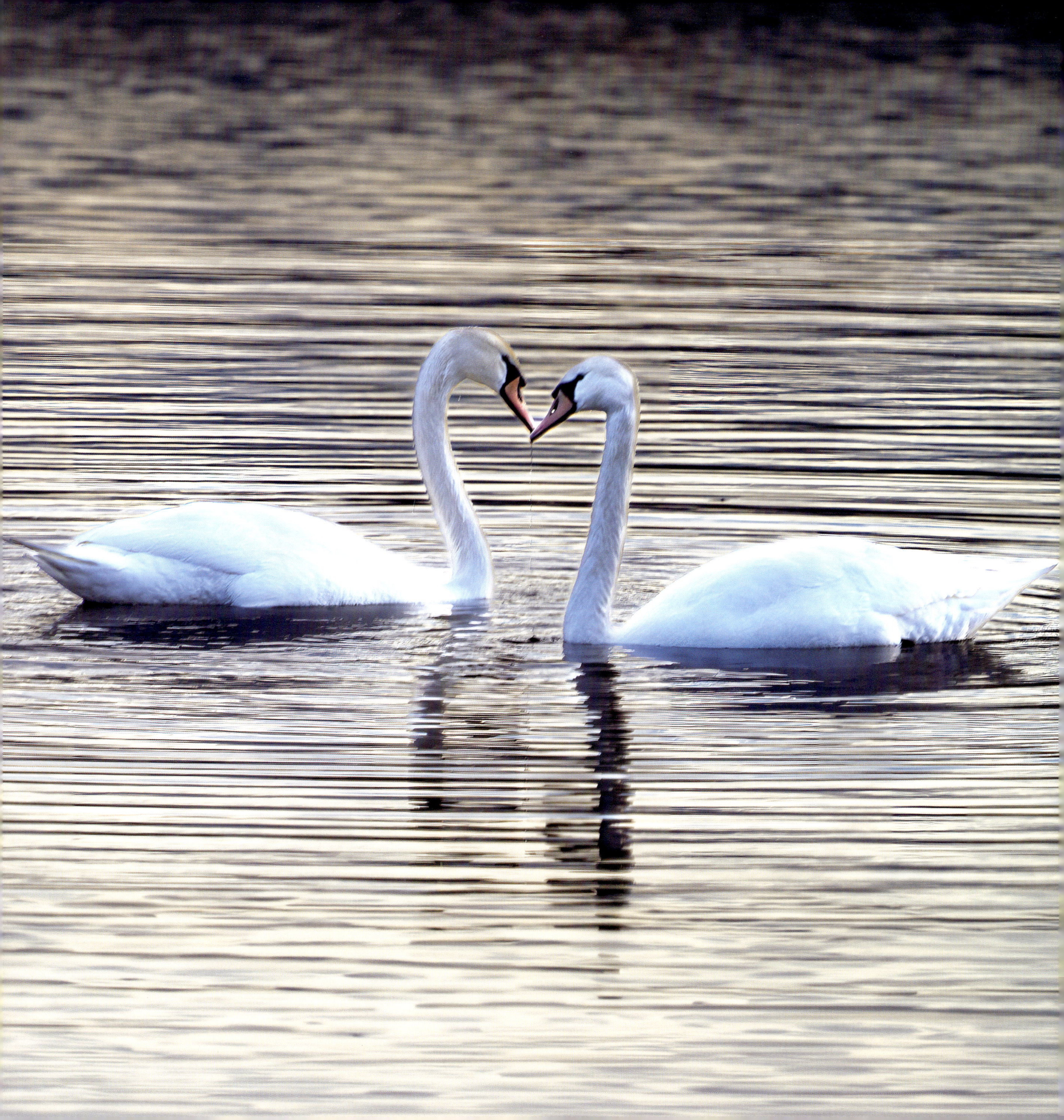

7.

Safe

This tiny vervet monkey has no idea that the world around him is dangerous; he just rests in the arms of his mother, safe and secure. The fact is she can't shield him from all the predators and dangers that surround him. But with new life, there is always hope. And for today, he is safe in his mother's arms.

I laid on the floor of our room in Zimbabwe and took a shot of this mom and baby through the sliding glass door of the balcony. They were two feet away.

VICTORIA FALLS SAFARI LODGE, ZIMBABWE | ISO 1000 | 105MM | 1/200

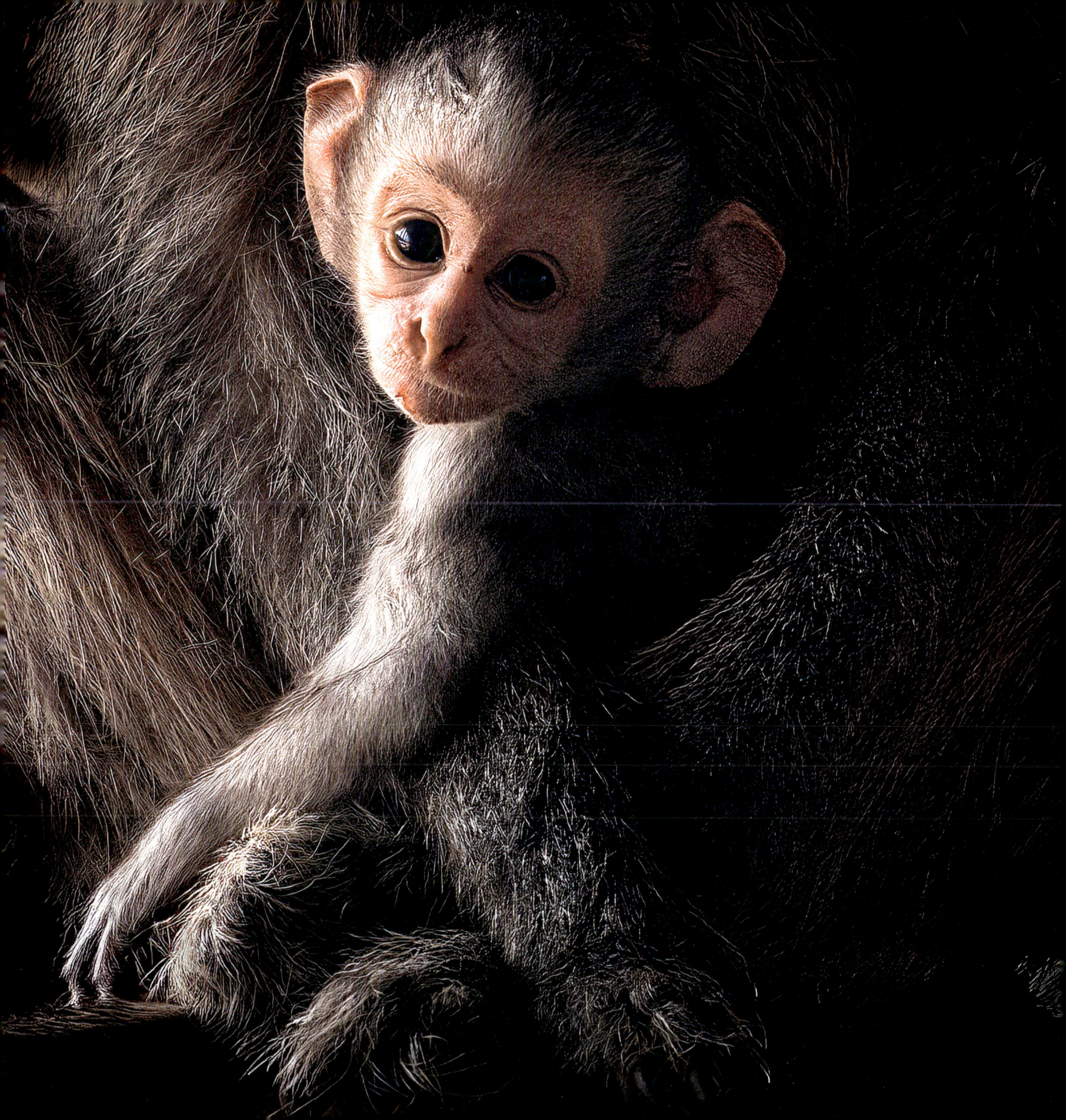

Dancing Beak to Beak

Great blue herons have their own dances, elaborate courtship rituals to select and woo a mate. As the herons settle in the nest, their courtship becomes more frenetic. It is quite a sight, with persistent clacking and snapping of bills; fluffing of feathers; poking, prodding, and pecking at each other; joint neck stretching; and various gyrations of heads, necks, and wings. The photos depict three distinct heron dance moves: the stretch, the cuddle, and the finale, dancing beak to beak. All these actions occur in a confined space, culminating in a precarious mating. As the dance advances, the female will grasp the male's bill in her own, indicating her acceptance of him, with mating soon to follow.

Last January, my father would have been 100 years old. The year he died, my parents had been married just shy of 65 years. Dad was a handsome Greek lad and Mom a beautiful Irish redhead. They met at a USO dance in 1942 just before Dad shipped out on a military troop transport. For the duration of the war, Dad and Mom courted via letters that crisscrossed the Pacific Ocean after clearing the censors. They married in 1947. The Greatest Generation loved to dance, and Mom and Dad were no exception.

The long legs and torsos of these birds as well as their high-altitude gymnastics evoke memories of Ginger Rogers and Fred Astaire skimming across the dance floor together in *Top Hat*, to

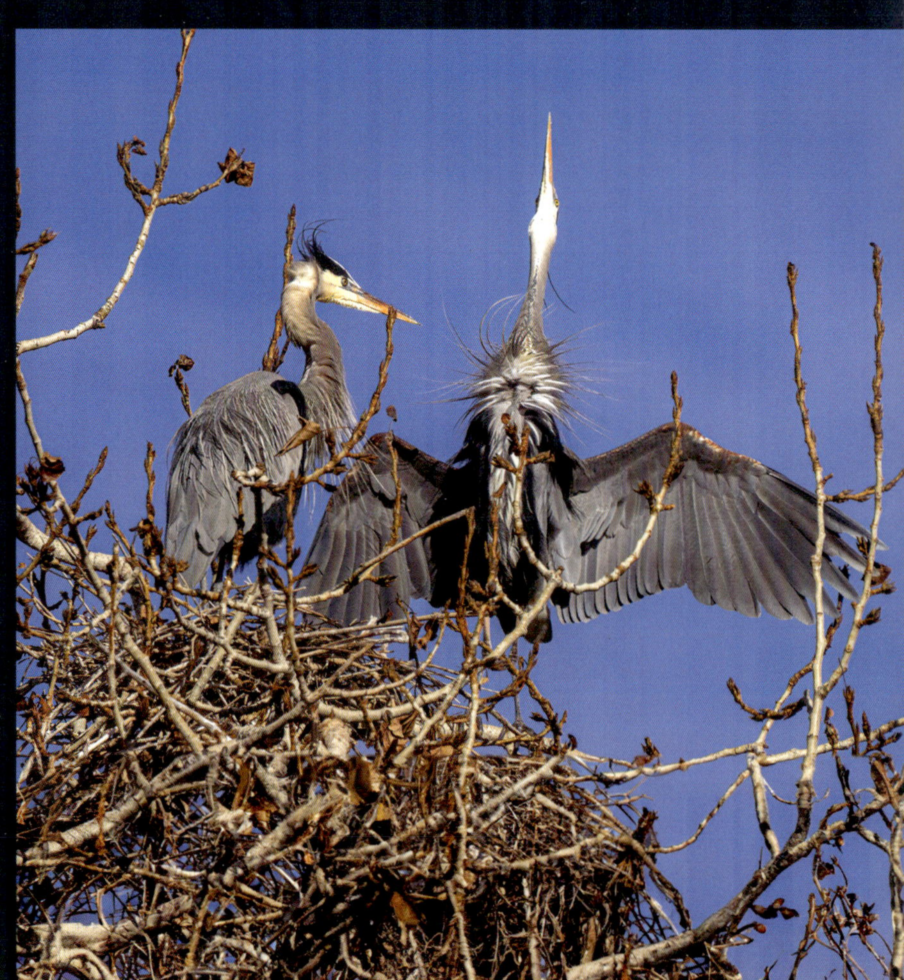

the words and melody of Irving Berlin's "Cheek to Cheek" (with a twist).

> *"Heaven, I'm in heaven*
> *And my heart beats so that I can hardly speak*
> *And I seem to find the happiness I seek*
> *When we're out together, dancing, beak to beak."*

I owe a lot of my creative writing skills to my Irish mother, who loved to tell me stories. And I owe my sense of the beauty and majesty of the world to my Greek father, who loved to take us fishing. Watching the great blue herons reminds me of them both. What reminds you of your parents?

Enduring freezing temperatures in January, I hunched under tree branches on the banks of the Boise River for days to catch these birds in the right poses. Wildlife photography requires both patience and perseverance.

EAGLE, IDAHO | ISO 400 | 840MM | 1/1600

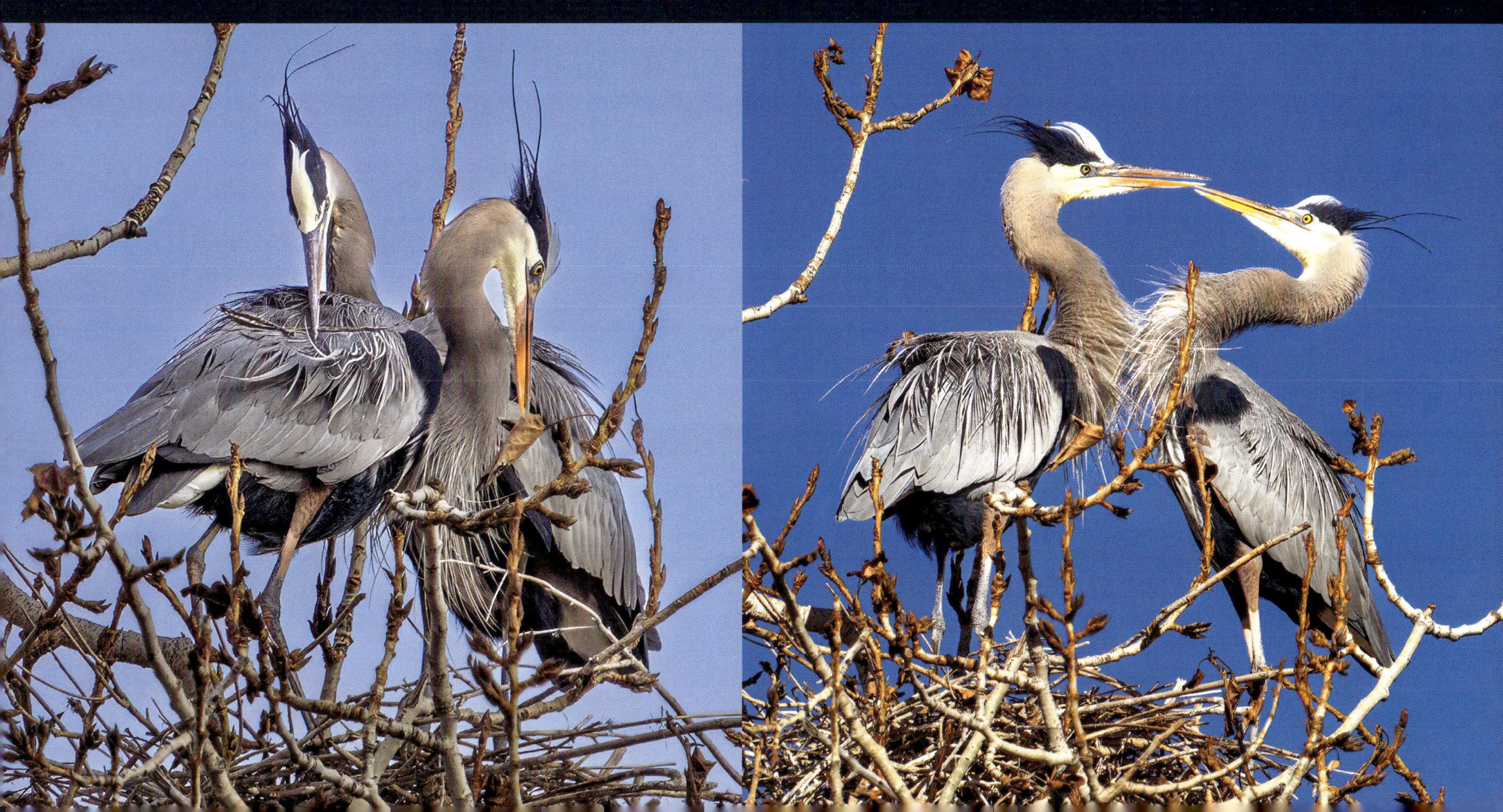

9.

Eye of the Tiger

In 1982, on the day before the release of the movie *Rocky II,* the English rock band Survivor released "Eye of the Tiger." The phrase is now an idiom for determination, courage, and focus to go the distance, or as the song repeats, "Just a man and his will to survive."

When I photograph wildlife, if at all possible, I want to capture their eyes. Creating an image with direct eye contact connects you with your subject. It instills an intimacy that brings the photo to life. The goal is to reveal the personality of the animal as well as its beauty. And as your eyes lock, you might wonder what is on its mind.

This is one of only two animals in captivity included in this book. The other is the endangered lemur. This tiger was in a half-acre enclosure in a wildlife park in Ontario, Canada.

ONTARIO, CANADA | ISO 500 | 500MM | 1/400

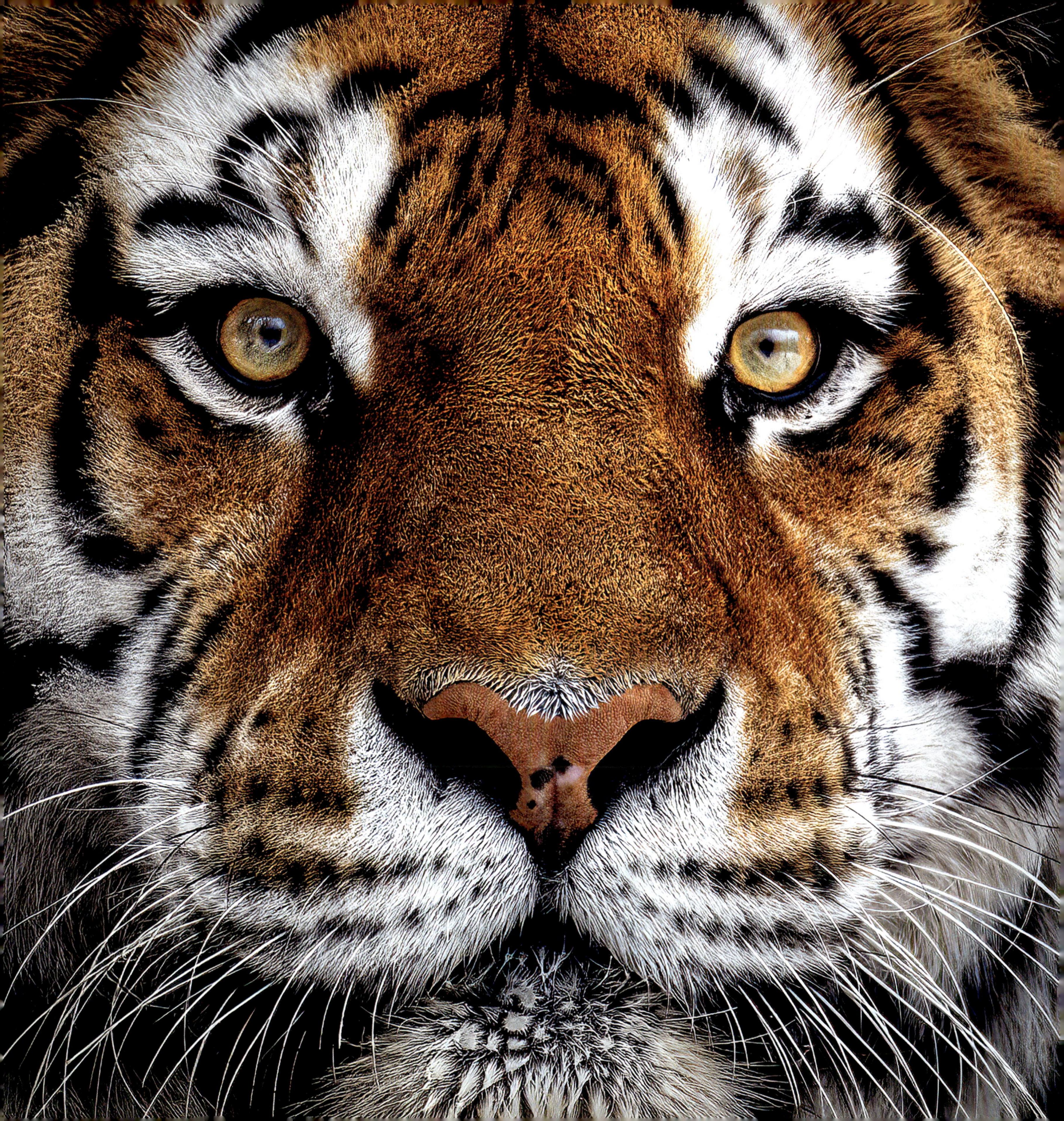

10.

"Price" Less

An eagle's eye fills almost a third of its face and dominates its features. Eyes set back on each side, the eagle has 340-degree vision. An eagle's stare is classic and unforgettable, mimicked only by the osprey in its intensity. It is darkly reminiscent of the unnerving Vincent Price stare I remember so well from Saturday nights growing up.

Saturday nights, our parents let us stay up late. We watched horror movies, though they were pretty tame in the 50s and 60s. My favorite was Lon Chaney in *The Wolfman.* But the creepy ones that made you sleep with the lights on always starred Vincent Price. He had that voice, look, and sinister stare that cut through you like a knife.

Back then, suspense was the heart of great horror movies. The characters were complex and memorable. I still cringe at the thought of *The Tomb of Ligeia*, *The Pit and the Pendulum*, or *The House on Haunted Hill.*

When this eagle stared down at me, it sent a little shiver up my spine, just like Vincent Price used to do.

I try to find negative space around my subjects. The goal of eliminating distractions is to direct your eye and focus to the subject.

BOISE RIVER, IDAHO | ISO 640 | 600MM | 1/3200

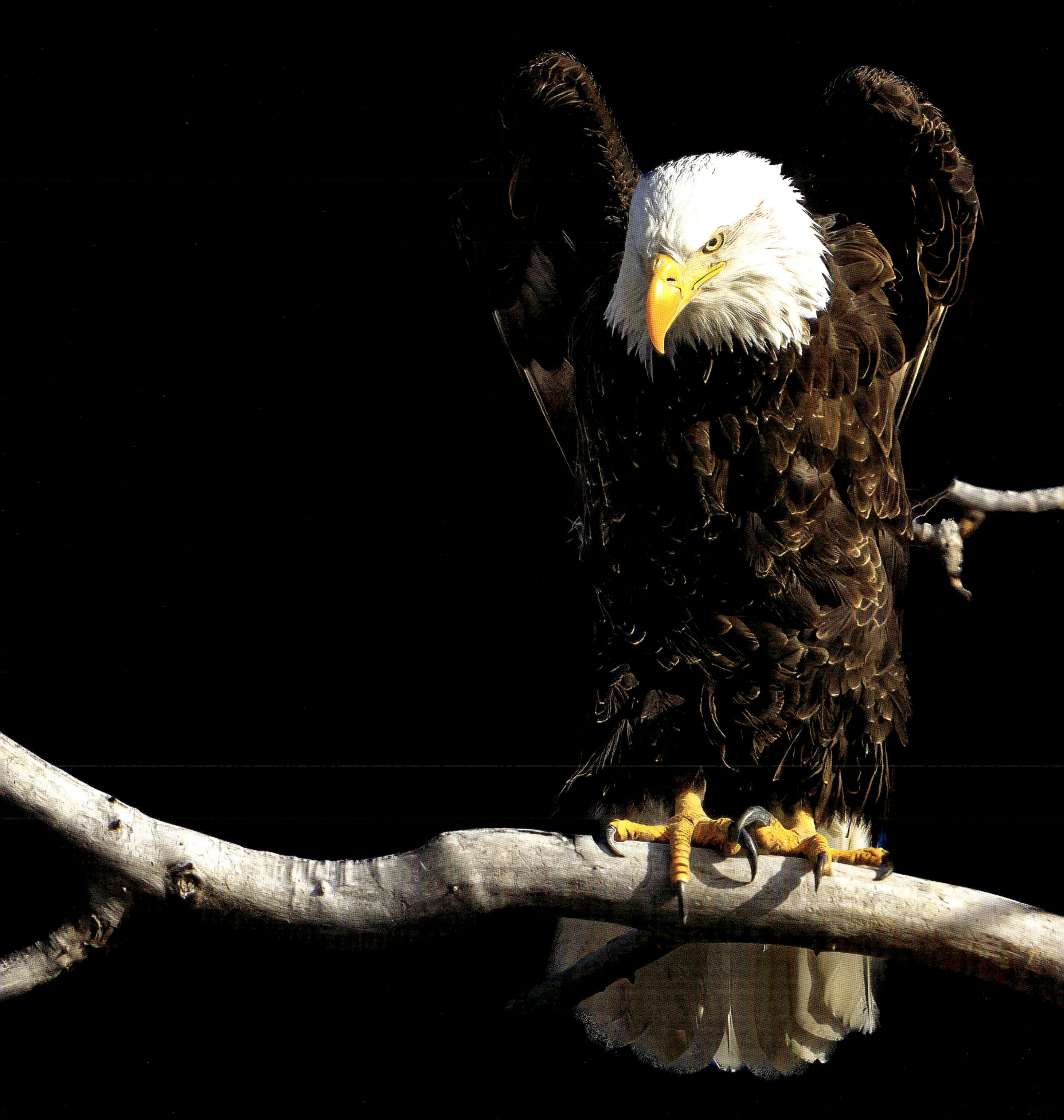

II.

Esau

In July 2021, Maureen and I took a trip of a lifetime—a safari to Kenya and Tanzania. More than any other animal, I wanted to photograph one of the last super tuskers, massive elephants whose tusks weigh up to 100 pounds apiece. The largest walking mammals on earth, there are less than 30 left in the world. Masai rangers are always somewhere close to the animals, keeping a vigilant lookout for ivory poachers who constantly hunt these rare, beautiful beasts.

A few years before we made our safari, a famous South African photographer was in Amboseli Park, Kenya, to photograph Esau, a particularly magnificent elephant with large tusks. I wanted to do the same. But not from the safety of a Land Rover. I wanted to be on the ground and close up. Was I a little crazy? Perhaps. But some things are worth the risk.

This shot was taken lying in the tall grass of the savannah. That is Esau, who stands about 10 feet tall and weighs 9,000 pounds. He is walking toward me from about 30 yards away. His frame filled my lens from top to bottom. After this shot, he was too close to get all of him in the picture.

For a few minutes, time slowed down; it was Esau and me—nothing else existed. Surprisingly, I was never afraid, though I can't say the same for Maureen or our guide.

Thankfully, nothing bad happened and I came home with my photo of a lifetime. I'm no adventure seeker and I knew this was risky. But if there's ever a chance to do this again, count me in.

A familiar subject can make a unique and compelling image viewed from a different perspective. In this case, what better way to emphasize the massive size of this elephant than seeing him from the ground beneath him.

AMBOSELI NP, KENYA | ISO 3200 | 275MM | 1/1000

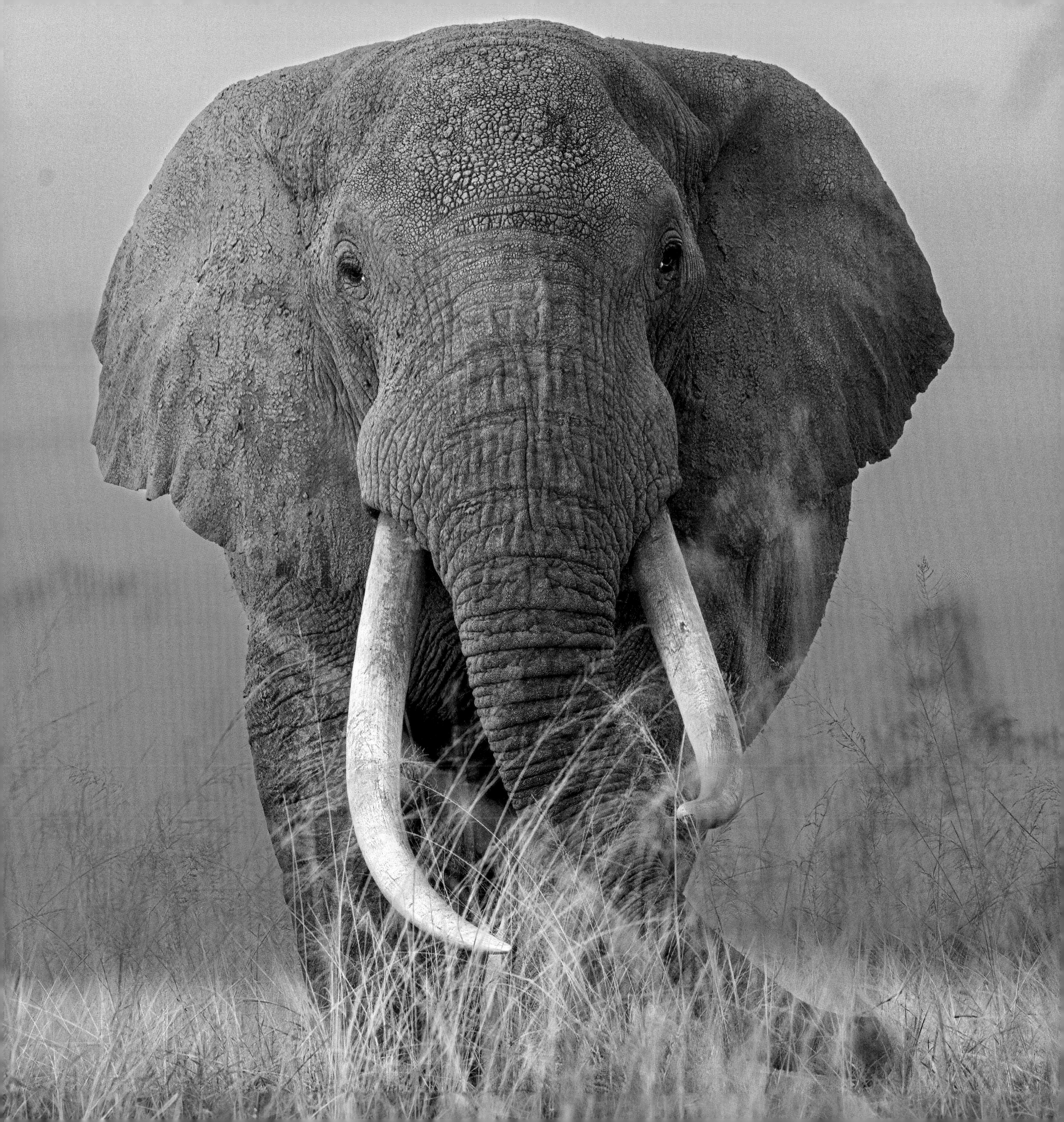

12.

The Early Bird

The robin's beautiful songs echo from the treetops. Early in the morning, you can watch them walking slowly through the grass, hunting night crawlers. Then you know that spring has arrived.

Dad started taking my brother Jim and me on fishing trips to Canada in 1962 when I was 10 years old. A week before we made the 13-hour drive from Illinois to Ontario, Canada, Jim and I were tasked with collecting night crawlers for the trip.

In the evening, we used the garden hose to soak the front and back yards. Then when it got dark out, we ventured into the yard on hands and knees with flashlights and coffee cans. The damp ground brought the night crawlers halfway out of their holes, but when the flashlight hit them, they retreated like a jack-in-the-box in reverse.

Our object was to grab them quickly and then carefully engage in a boy-to-worm tug of war. The trick was to pull just enough to coax the worm out of its tunnel without tearing it apart. We had a keen sense of a worm's elasticity limits, having honed our skills by countless hours spent stretching red licorice strips in our spare time.

Sixty years and nearly 50 fishing trips later, the night crawler harvest days are still vivid to me. Our dad's love for fishing with his kids left us with happy memories that will endure for a lifetime.

Time is the one thing in life you can't get back. Gifting your children with special memories of time spent together doing what you love is the best investment you could ever make in their lives.

While horizontal and vertical lines in photographs project stability and strength, a diagonal creates tension. With a common subject like a robin, use of a diagonal and placement of the subject off-center creates a more interesting composition.

GARDEN CITY, IDAHO | ISO 1600 | 600MM | 1/500

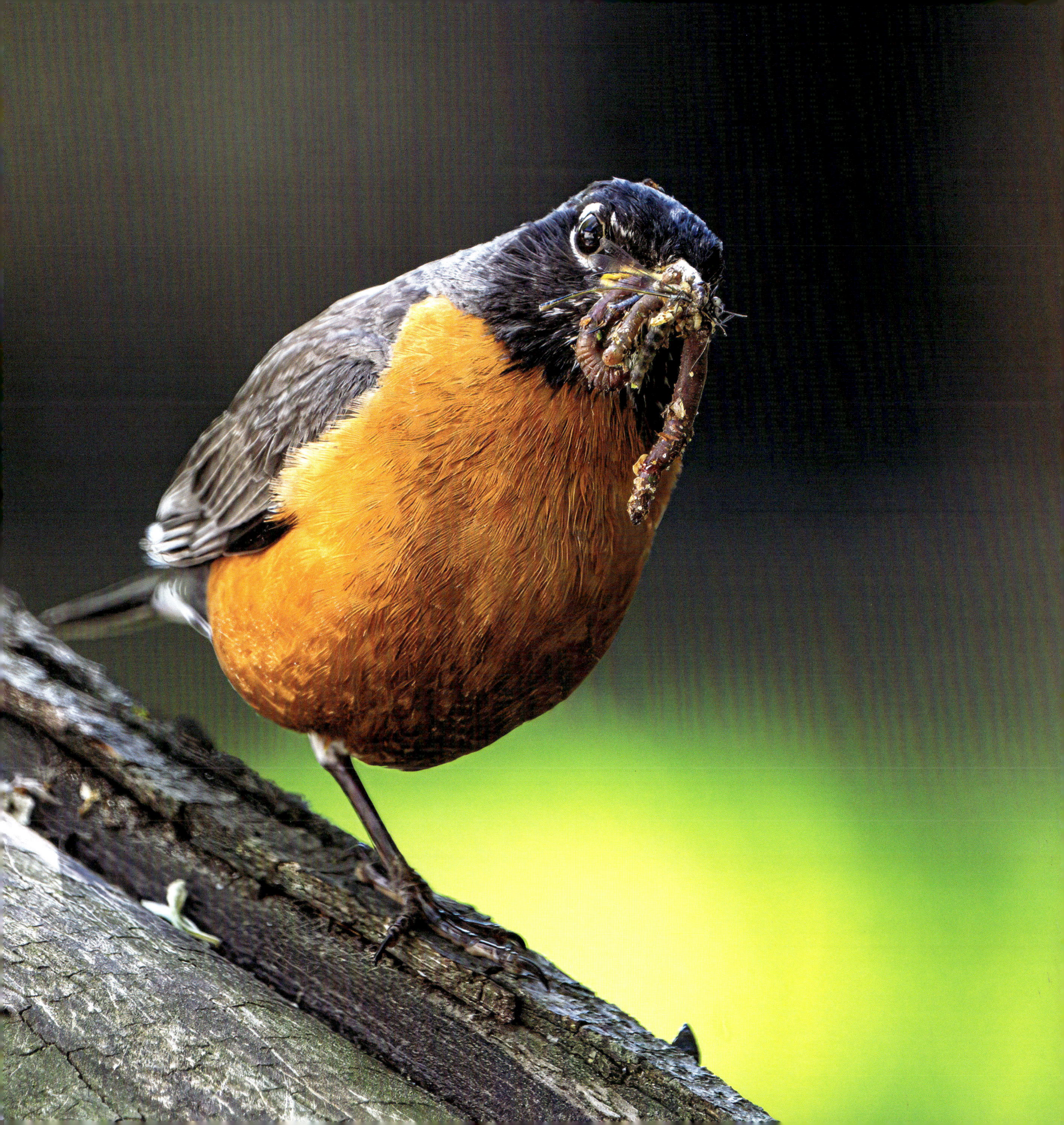

13.

Aslan

This is Rodrigo, king of the Sand River lion pride in Kenya's Masai Mara. According to the Masai people, he is the only lion known to carry a unique and distinctive birthmark on his forehead—a cross.

On a chilly morning in July, we left our safari camp before sunrise to drive across the African plains in search of the Sand River pride. This photo was taken from 30 feet away as the lions basked in the early morning sun, having just feasted on the nearby carcass of a wildebeest killed the night before.

Thirty-five hundred years ago, Moses wrote in Genesis about the coming Messiah who would save mankind from their sins. He was called the Lion of Judah (Genesis 49). In *The Chronicles of Narnia*, the famous theologian C.S. Lewis tells the story of Aslan, a lion who surrenders his life to free the world from an eternal winter. Four hundred years before Jesus was born in Bethlehem, the prophet Isaiah predicted that the Lion of Judah would do just that: willingly give his life to save us all (Isaiah 53).

The serene face of this majestic lion evokes a mental picture of Jesus in the Garden of Gethsemane the night before he went to the cross. There, Jesus prayed these words for us:

"I am praying not only for these disciples but also for all who will ever believe in me through their message. I pray that they will all be one, just as you and I are one—as you are in me, Father, and I am in you. And may they be in us so that the world will believe you sent me." John 17:20-21 (NLT)

All of us have moments in our lives when God's presence is palpable and powerful. This was one of mine.

Just after sunrise, our open Range Rover was creeping slowly past the pride. I waited until we passed on the lion's right side to capture the light across his right eye and forehead, with his left side in shadow.

MASAI MARA NP, KENYA | ISO 250 | 437MM | 1/250

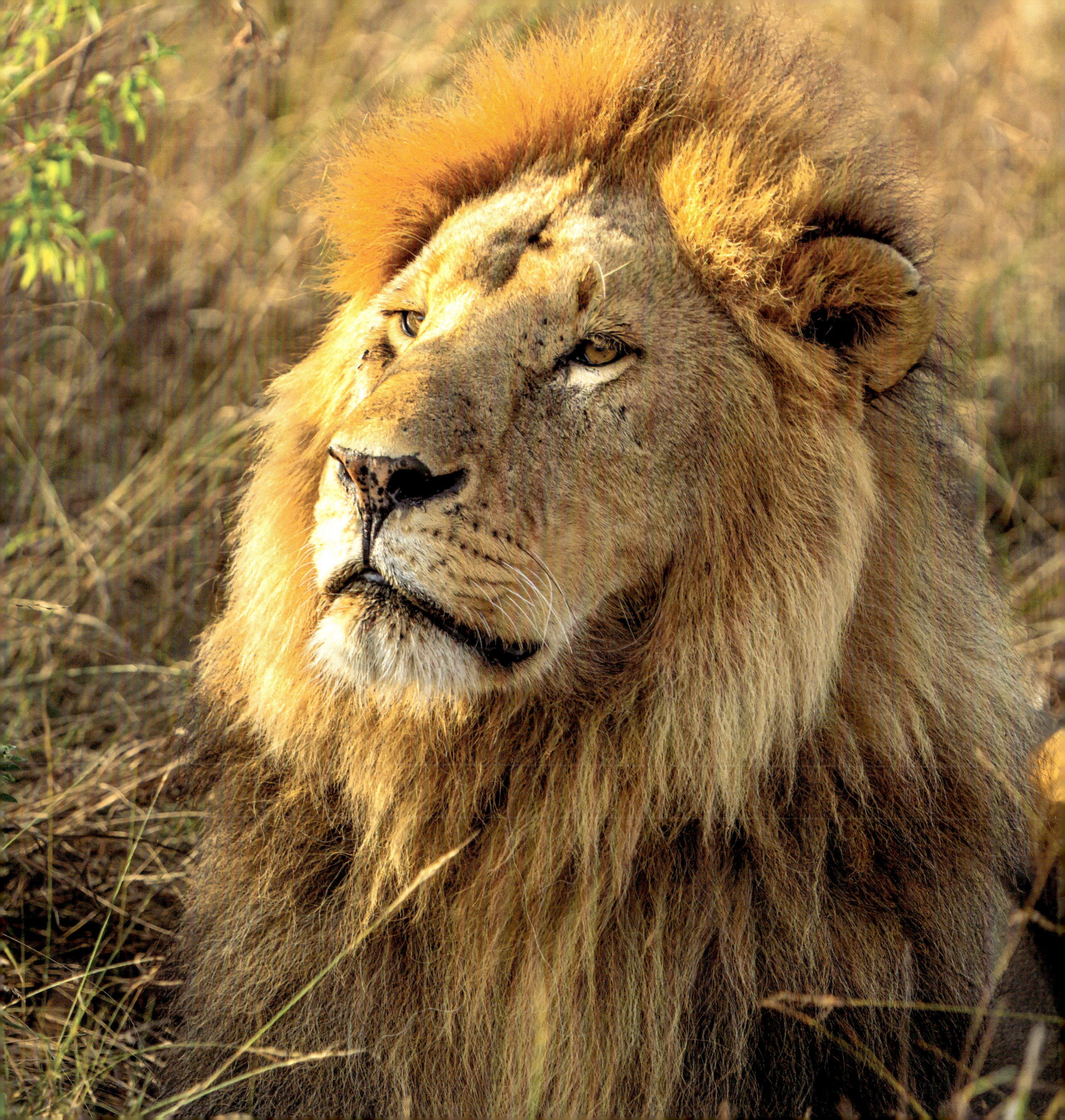

14.

Here's Lookin' at You

A cardinal rule of wildlife photography is never disturb the animal. Here, in the excitement of the moment, I stumbled onto two bald eagles on the banks of Alaska's Kenai River. Their calm reaction surprised me.

Typically, a bird startled by sound or movement flies off without hesitation. After all, danger is everywhere. Even though bald eagles are apex predators at the top of the food chain, they still have natural enemies, including wildcats, coyotes, larger birds like vultures, and of course, humans.

Nor did they overlook my presence. An eagle's eyesight is four to five times superior to ours and its eyes are positioned 30 degrees away from the center of its face, providing it with a far wider field of vision. An eagle can spot a rabbit miles away. That's what we call an "eagle eye."

So, instead of leaving, one eagle turned to look directly at me while the other eagle surveyed their flank. I didn't move. For 30 seconds, we simply regarded each other. Then, they calmly flew off.

Only later did I make sense out of it all. In my neck of the woods, Boise, Idaho, only a few eagles spend the winter, and they are wary. But it seems that in Alaska, eagles, which are abundant, have become acclimated to people. As the saying goes, "Familiarity breeds contempt."

Man's interactions with birds and wildlife haven't always worked out well. While I was enthralled with the opportunity to watch these beautiful birds watching me up close, I fear that by becoming comfortable around humans, the Alaskan eagle may unwittingly be courting disaster.

This photo was taken lying on a beach 10 yards from the shoreline. A group of eagles were fighting over fish carcasses when this pair landed. My presence was immediately observed but I was quiet and remained immobile.

KENAI RIVER, ALASKA | ISO 2000 | 280MM | 1/2500

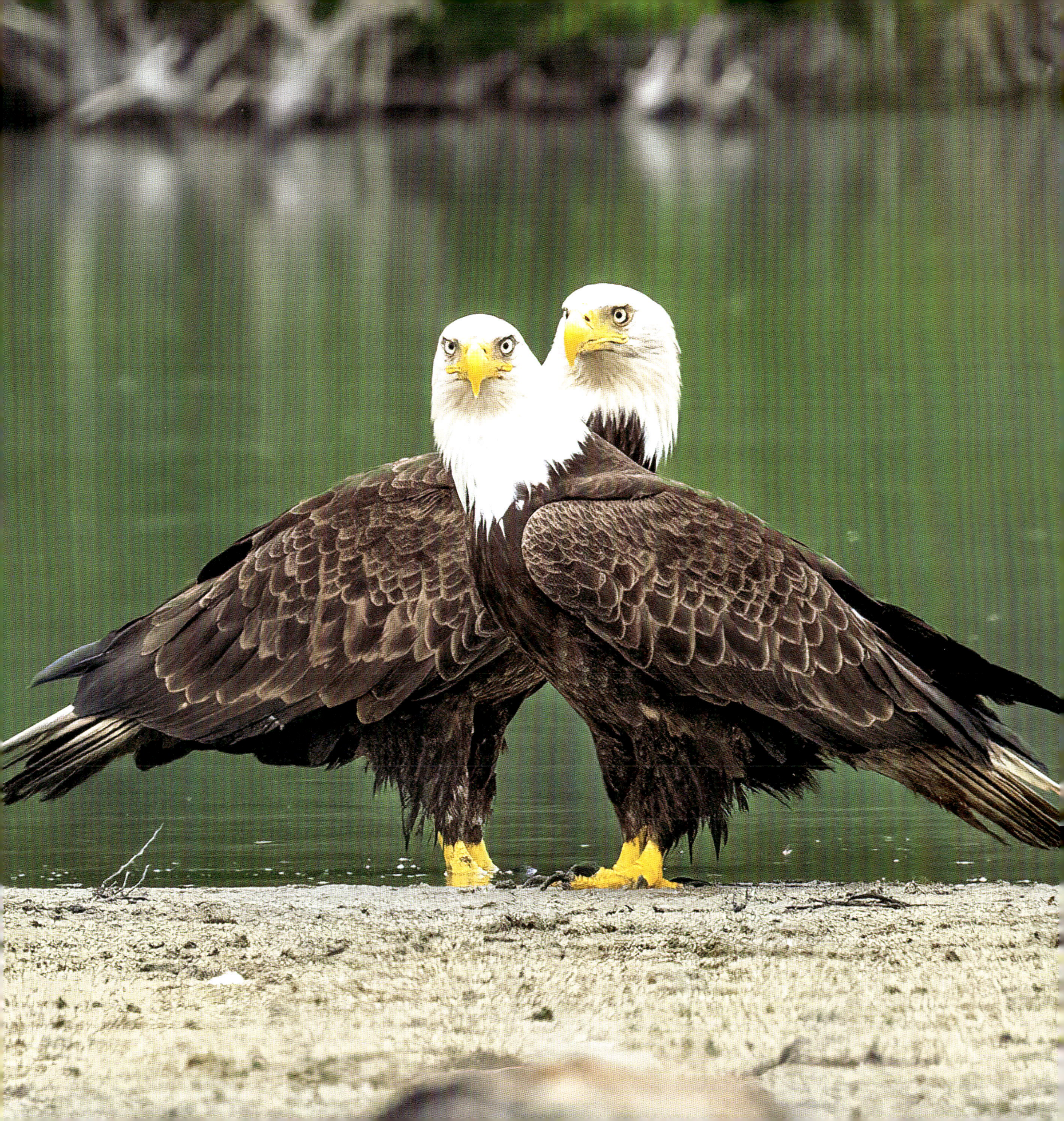

15.

Band of Brothers

These three cheetahs resting in the shade are brothers. Their mother was watching from several yards away.

Cheetahs have no natural ability to hunt. They must be trained, first by a parent, and then with their brothers, working together as a team. Cheetahs are known for their blazing speed, up to 70 miles an hour in under four seconds. But it is their stealth, strategy, and teamwork that makes them formidable.

I watched four cheetahs startle a herd of wildebeest, cull a lone straggler, outflank it, and then take turns harrying it until one was close enough to pounce on its neck and bring it down.

My brother and I and our brother-in-law Stew were all trial lawyers. We've had a lifetime of battles in court, and our fair share of victories and defeats. When we worked together, I brought passion and heart to the mix, Stew was a workhorse with an eye for detail, and Jim was the general, a consummate tactician and brilliant legal mind. Together, we made a great team.

The phrase "band of brothers" was coined by William Shakespeare. He wrote of King Henry V's famous St. Crispin's Day speech, given to his men on the eve of the Battle of Agincourt. The British were far outnumbered by the French, but still managed to win, ending the Hundred Years' War between England and France.

Just like the trio of Jim, Stew, and me—brothers through thick and thin—there's no rivalry among these cheetahs. Instead, there's an unquestioned reliance on each other's skill, heart, and fidelity, truly a band of brothers.

When you see an odd number of subjects in a photo, your brain must work hard to organize them, which makes the composition more interesting. The rule of odds says, whenever possible, a composition should have an odd number of objects.

SERENGETI NP, TANZANIA | ISO 800 | 200MM | 1/2000

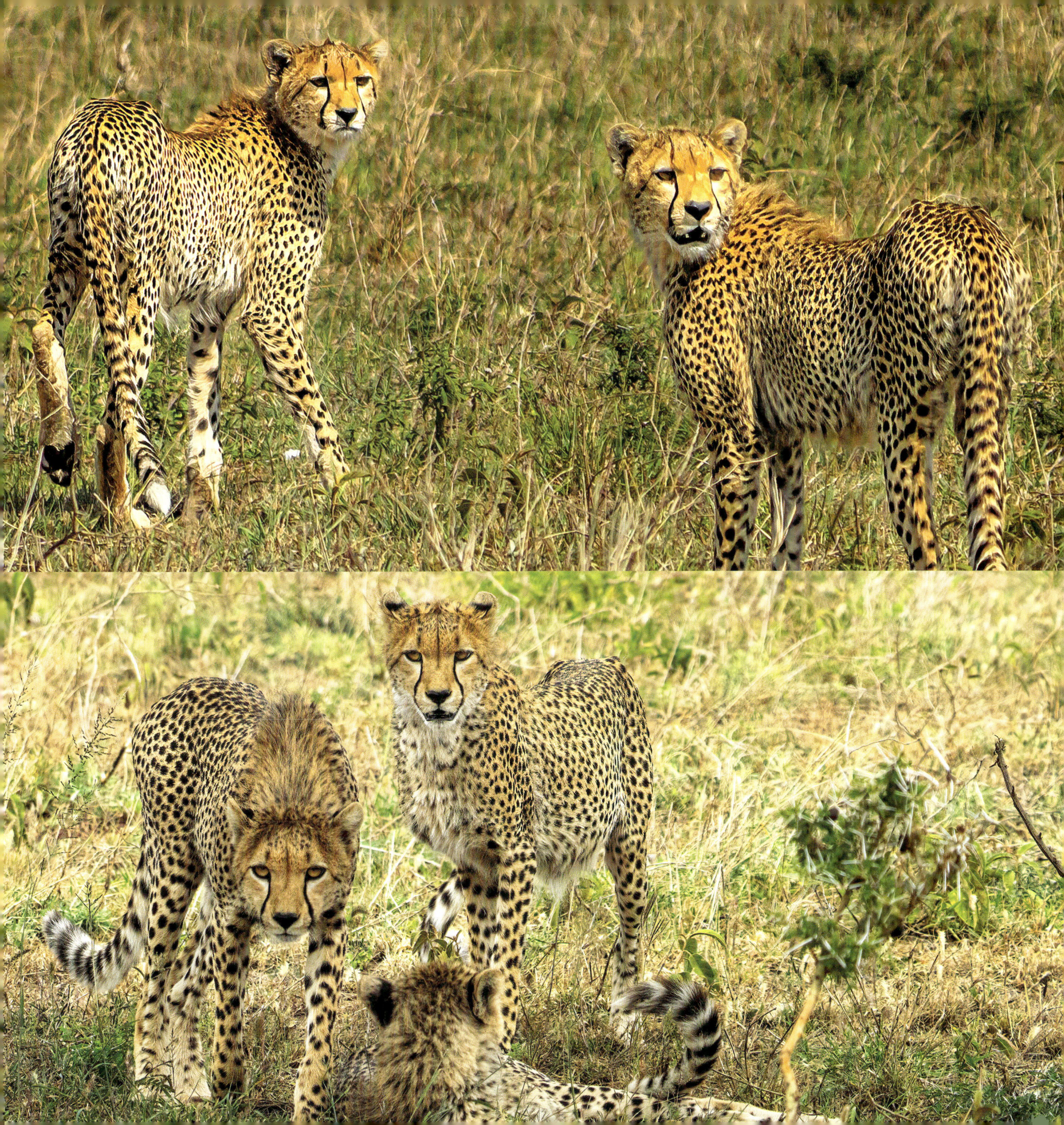

16.

Wild

These magnificent mustangs roam the expanses of the mountains surrounding the Snake River in southwestern Idaho.

The wild mustang is featured in the movie *Hidalgo*. It romanticizes the life of Frank T. Hopkins, a cowboy who performed in Buffalo Bill's *Wild West* show. In the movie, an Arabian sheikh dares him to enter the Ocean of Fire race across the unforgiving Sahara. Hopkins rides his mustang, Hidalgo, against purebred Arabian stallions in the treacherous race and, of course, wins.

No one knows if the story is true since Hollywood often exaggerates or rewrites history. Regardless, the movie gives a fitting salute to this incredible icon of the Old West.

Ancestors of the wild mustangs were brought to America by the Spanish. Some of their domesticated horses escaped, originating these feral herds. I heard stories about them long ago, but it was 60 years later that I saw them in person. My friend Joe and I walked three miles through sagebrush until we caught up with a herd of about 30. While I was preoccupied taking photos, two stallions, sentries for the herd, sidled closer to us with the rest trailing behind. Suddenly, we realized we were surrounded. That's when we decided it was time to skedaddle.

Standing in the Idaho mountains in the midst of this herd of wild mustangs was a rare treat, virtual time travel to days of yesteryear, and a pleasant momentary diversion from the creeping curse of civilization.

The first rule for photographing any wild animal is never to be alone. Someone must watch the animals you don't see while you're focused on your subject. Joe saved my bacon by warning me that the other horses were starting to surround me.

MURPHY, IDAHO | ISO 400 | 840MM | 1/500

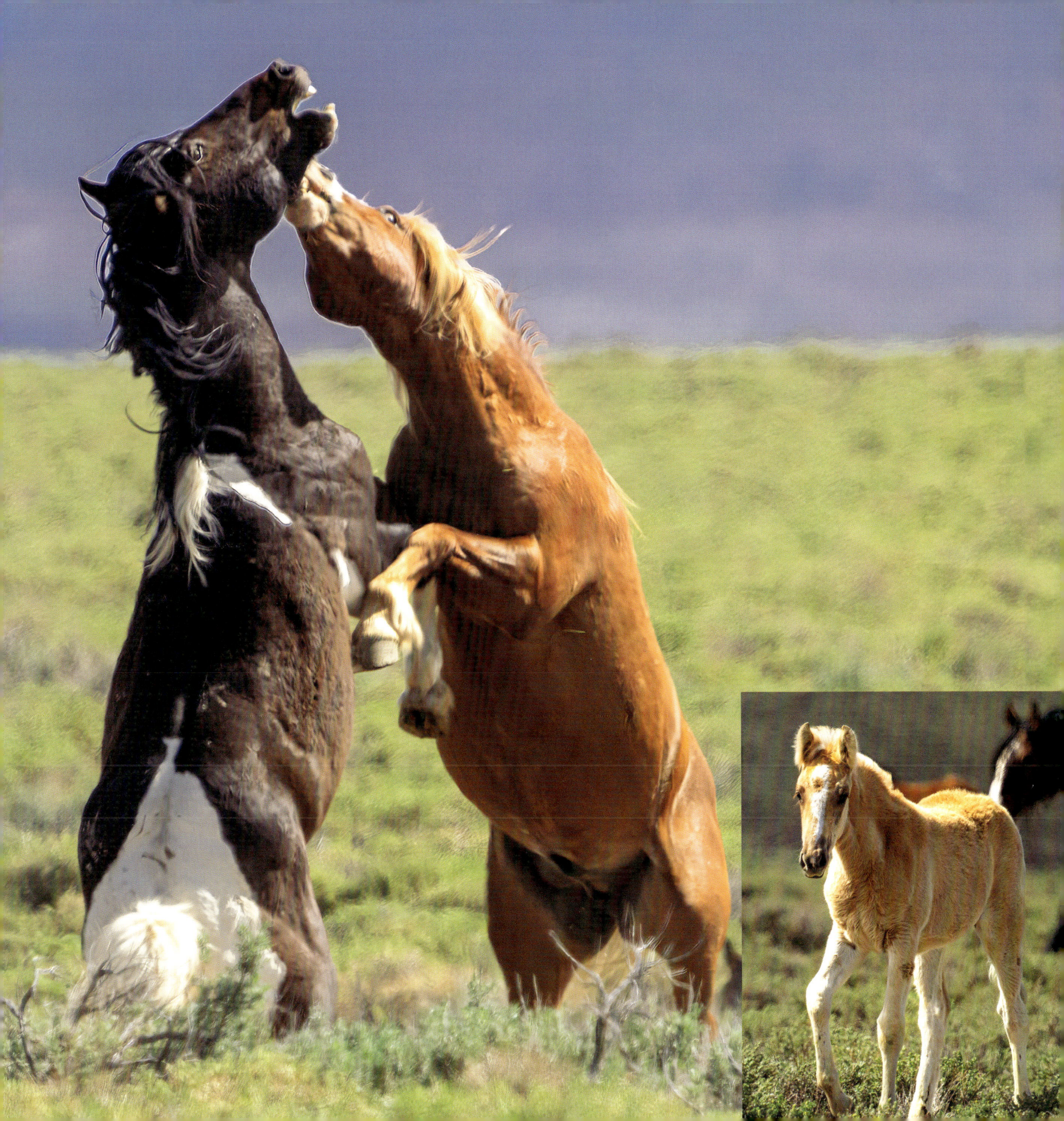

17.

Fairies

Blooming spring flowers bring these hummingbirds home to Idaho. When bugs become scarce and flowers no longer bloom in late August, they will depart, flying thousands of miles to Central and South America.

I was confined to home with a bad cold when these hummers arrived. Sometimes they buzz up to your face and look you right in the eye, motionless in the air. Their iridescent bodies and the blur of their wings, moving 10-80 times a second, conjure images of the flights of fairies, or as the Irish call them, the fair folk.

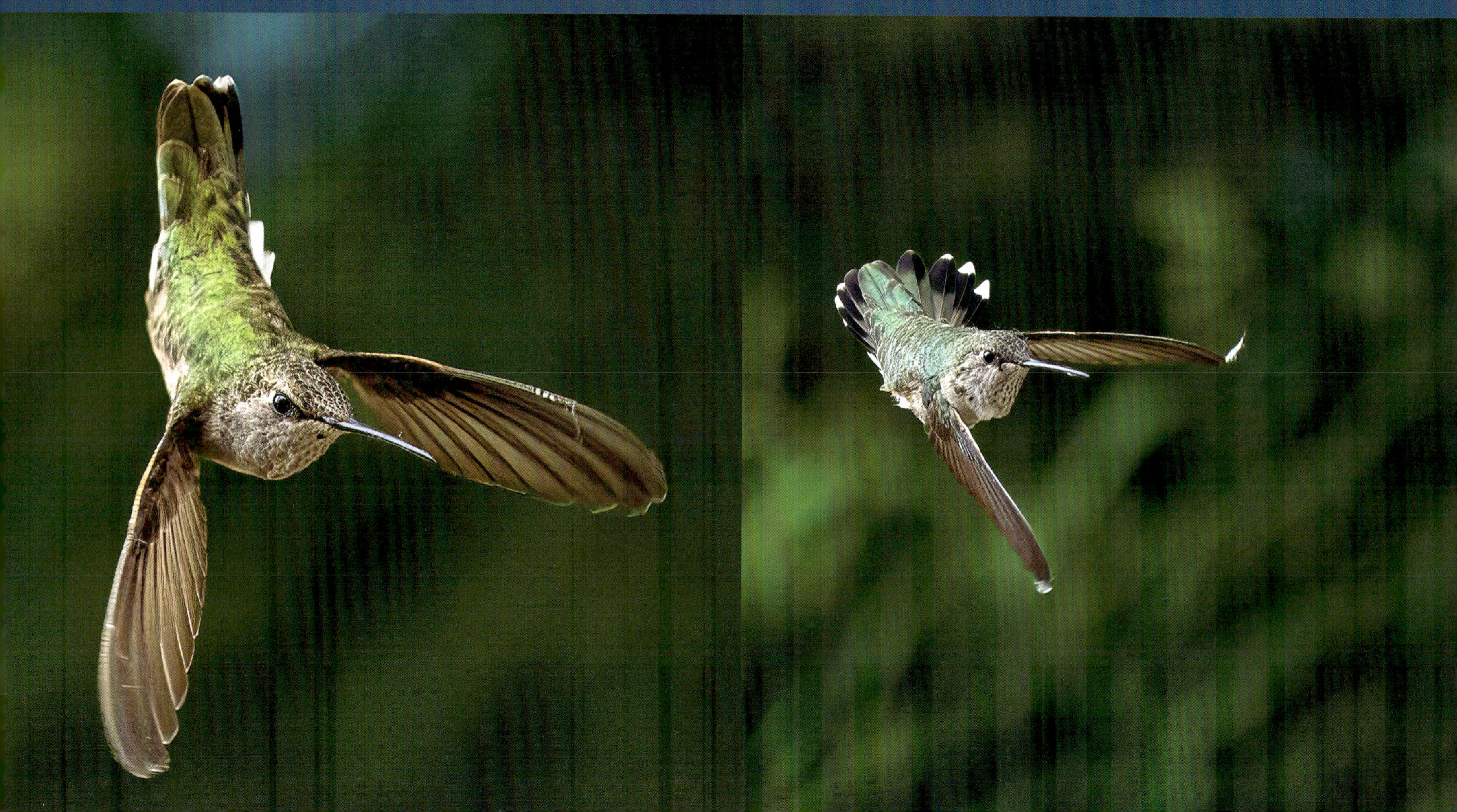

The most famous of the fairies is of course Tinker Bell, Peter Pan's tiny helper in J.M. Barrie's 1911 children's classic *Peter and Wendy*. After Peter Pan's literary debut, fairies would often be pictured as little, flying, mischievous, but well-meaning, imps, glowing and bustling about on tiny gossamer wings.

Among the acts of Christian love lauded in the Bible, Matthew's Gospel includes, "I was sick and you visited me." Matthew 25:36 (NKJV) Although I don't believe in fairies, the presence of these little flying diamonds was a pinch of pixie dust for me. When you aren't feeling well, nothing is better than a friend's company, human or otherwise.

Whenever possible, I prefer to use a tripod for wildlife photography. It allows me to take clear and detailed photos. Hummingbirds are an exception because they zip around erratically. Following them is easier with the camera in my hand.

BOISE, IDAHO | ISO 1600 | 110MM | 1/4000

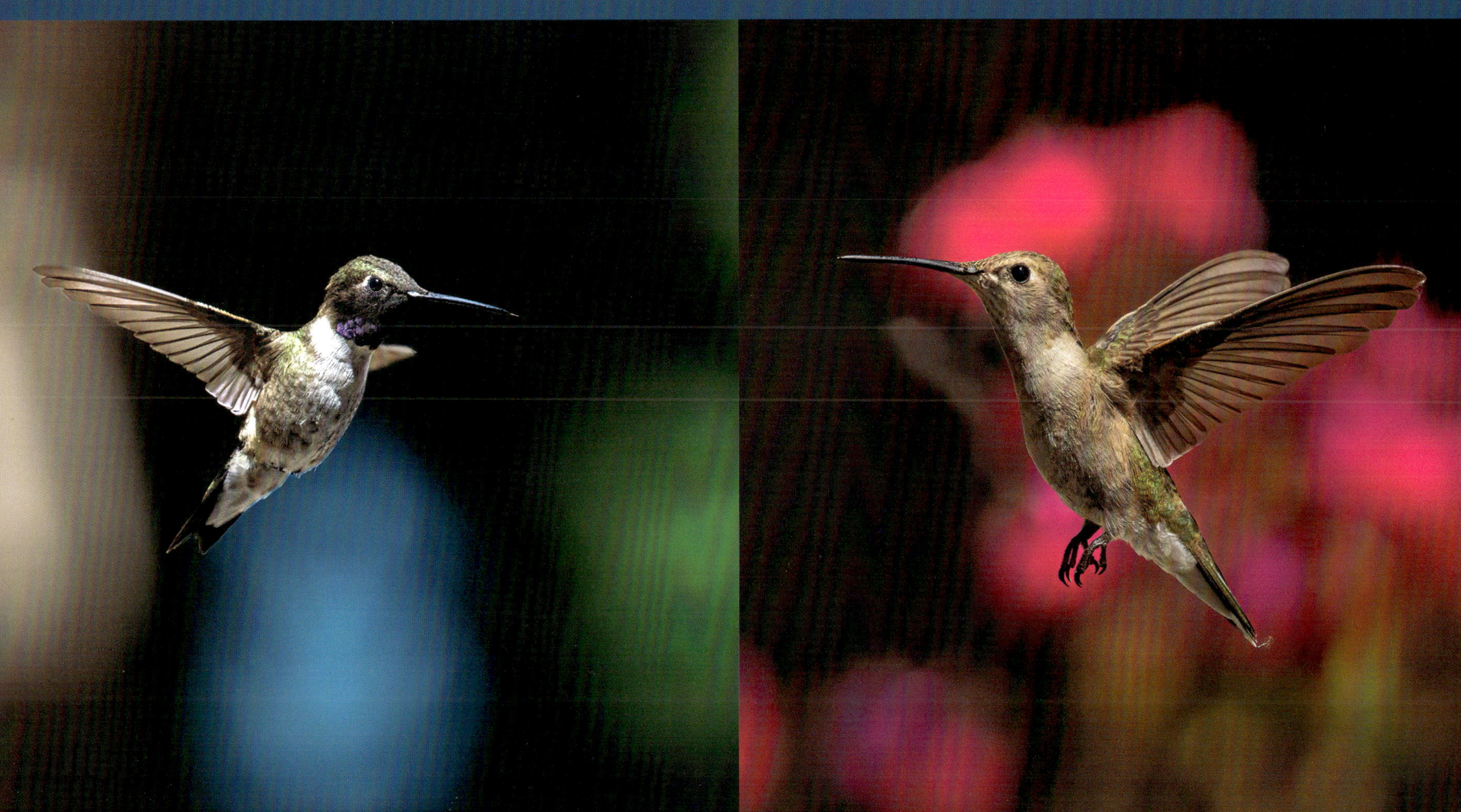

18.

On the Nose

When a lioness gives birth to her cubs, she leaves the pride and has her babies in a secluded spot. She keeps them away from the rest of the pride until they are about three months old. By then, they can keep up with the rest and muscle their way to a meal from one of the lactating females in the pride. Any lioness will suckle a cub within the pride, even if it is not her own.

This lion cub still needs a helpful boost. In this case, he gets across a rivulet of a stream helped by a nose—Momma's nose.

The other photo shows another helpful boost. This time, my mother is holding me aloft while I hold a fishing pole at the banks of Indian Creek near Earlville, Illinois. I was 5 months old. It was May 1952—over 70 years ago.

Dad took every Thursday off to go fishing. Sometimes, Mom accompanied him. Until I could stand up and cast a line for myself, she was my personal booster seat. She retained that post for the rest of her life. I could always call Mom and talk about important things, or nothing at all; we did just that for an hour or more at least once a week until she passed in 2015.

I credit my Irish Mom with my love of a good story. She was always ready with one, sometimes poignant and wise, sometimes sweet and tender, sometimes just silly, but always shared with a healthy dose of laughter and always with love.

No matter your age, everyone needs a boost from time to time. Moms are always there to lift you up.

Without a wide-angle lens, I lost the tip of this lion's tail because our guide and driver kept our vehicle close to the animals for the sake of my fellow travelers taking photos with their cell phones.

MASAI MARA NP, KENYA | ISO 3200 | 200MM | 1/2500

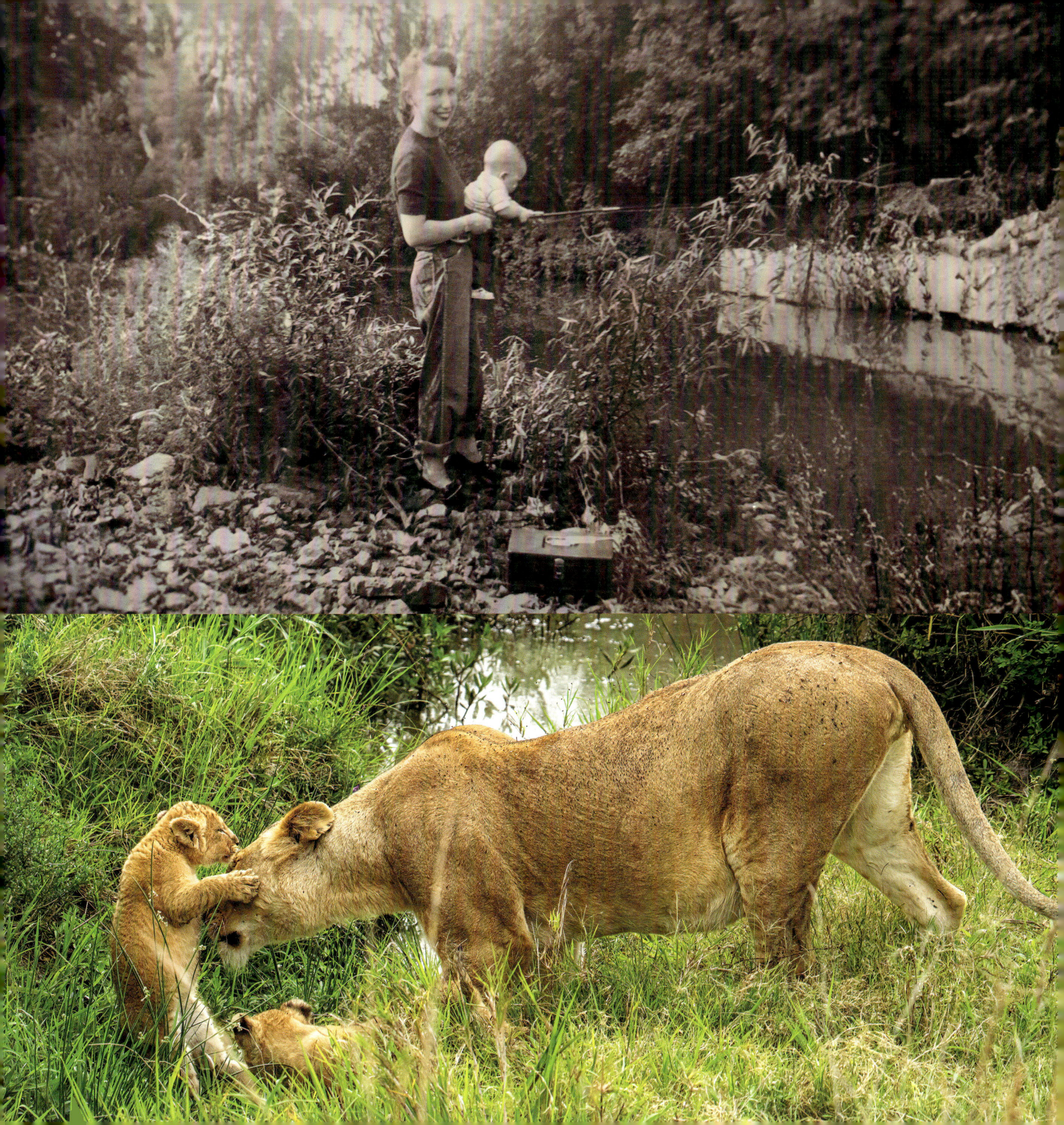

19.

Fidgety Fussbudgets

These two owlets are about 7 weeks old. The freedom of flight is still an elusive dream.

I remember the days before I gained my freedom. I grew up with three sisters and one brother. Our family took long road trips in a station wagon, camping at parks around the country. Imagine four (and when our youngest sister, Ann, arrived, five) restless kids in the back of a hot car (no air-conditioning) on long drives through the Black Hills, Badlands, Rocky Mountains, and countless other destinations across the Midwest and West. Mom and Dad constantly heard the same refrains from the backseat: "I want the window seat—it's my turn," "He's in my space," "She's picking on me," "Stop hitting me," and the ever-recurring theme, "I need to go to the bathroom."

Eventually, Dad would tire of our endless bickering and threaten, "If I have to stop this car, I'll give you something to cry about!" But we knew he was mostly bluff and bluster, so after a few minutes of awkward silence, one of us would start up again, surreptitiously poking his little sister, Diana, until she gave out the desired response: "Mom, Christ is poking me." At that point, I would vehemently declare my innocence and then blame my brother Jim, who was quietly minding his own business, in the window seat, of course.

All these little owlets can do right now is sit on the branches of the great cottonwood tree they call home, flap their untested wings, and wait for Mom or Dad to bring them dinner. With nothing but time on their hands (in this case, wings) and boredom inevitably setting in, kids will be kids. Mom used to call us "fidgety fussbudgets," words that ring true across every species.

Knowing I needed an unusual perspective, I walked directly underneath these owls and over-exposed the image by two-thirds of a stop to illuminate the texture of the tree bark as well as the owlets' feathers.

BOISE RIVER GREENBELT, IDAHO | ISO 800 | 600MM | 1/2500

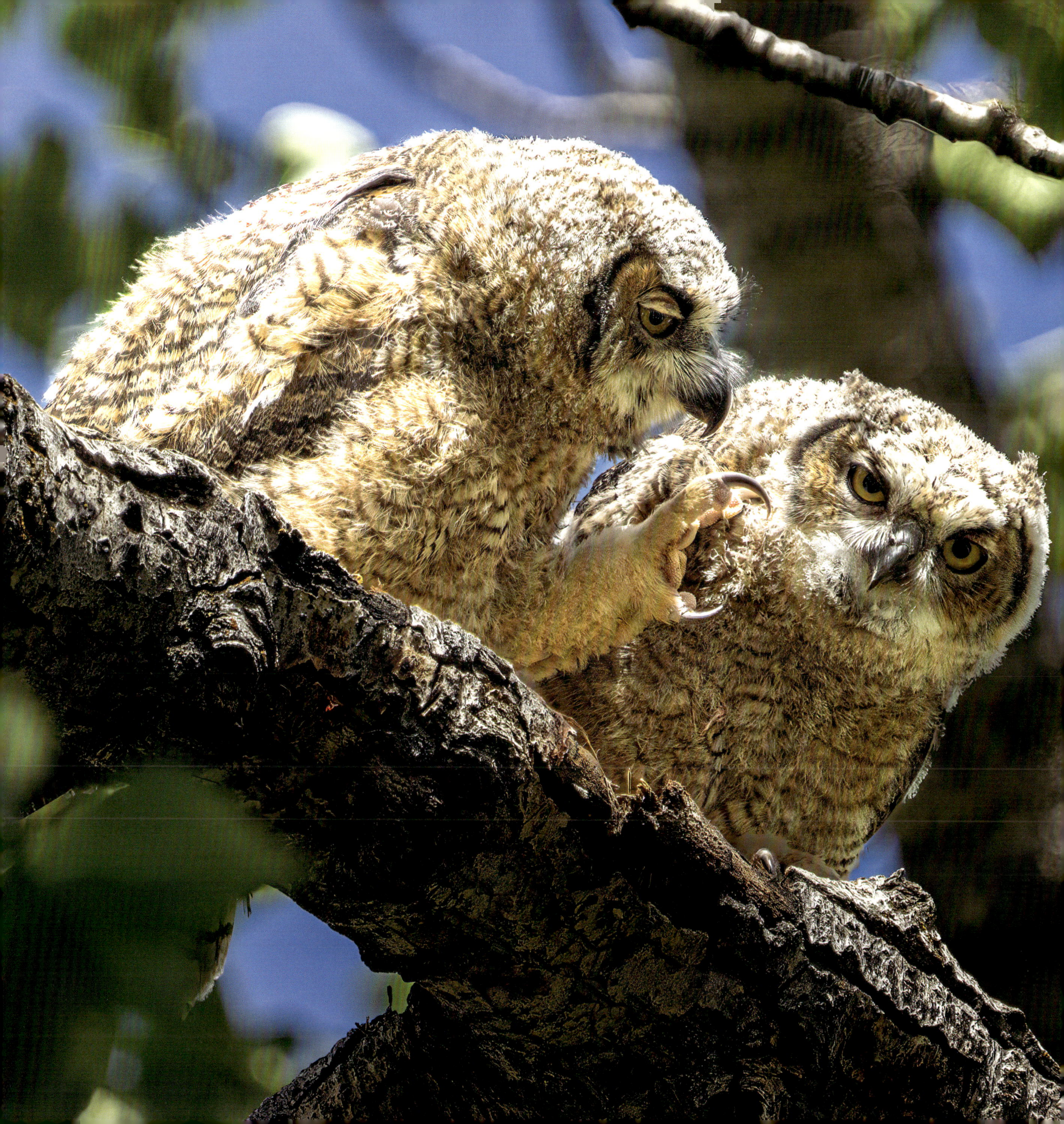

20. Stripes

Zebras are so prevalent across Africa that you hardly notice them, even though they are among the most beautiful and exotic of African wildlife. In fact, they are my wife's favorite.

Scientists have long known that each zebra's stripes are as unique as a fingerprint. No two patterns are alike. That fact has allowed them to identify and study individual zebras in large herds in the wild.

Are zebras white with black stripes or black with white stripes? A famed biologist studying zebras concluded that they are black with white stripes.

As to why they have stripes, it could be that biting flies don't often land on striped surfaces; they fail to decelerate and bounce off. Or it might be that stripes regulate heat. Black stripes absorb it to warm the zebra in the morning while white stripes reflect the sun while they graze in the afternoons. Scientists are still gathering data on whether a zebra's stripes create "motion dazzle" to confuse predators.

What is undeniable is that each one-of-a-kind zebra is wonderfully and intelligently designed, not the random product of chance. Moreover, the zebra is not the lone example. Every species tells the same story.

The probability that our universe and all life within it was created by chance and not by an intelligent Creator has been calculated by scientists to be 1 in 120 billion. To put that in perspective, if you bought one lottery ticket, you would have to win the lottery 120 billion times in a row to beat those odds.

The intricate and purposeful design of a zebra's stripes is proof enough for me that they didn't get here by chance, and I thank God for that.

The autofocus in your camera needs light and contrast to work well. The zebra's stripes provide just that contrast.

SERENGETI NP, TANZANIA | ISO 500 | 338MM | 1/1000

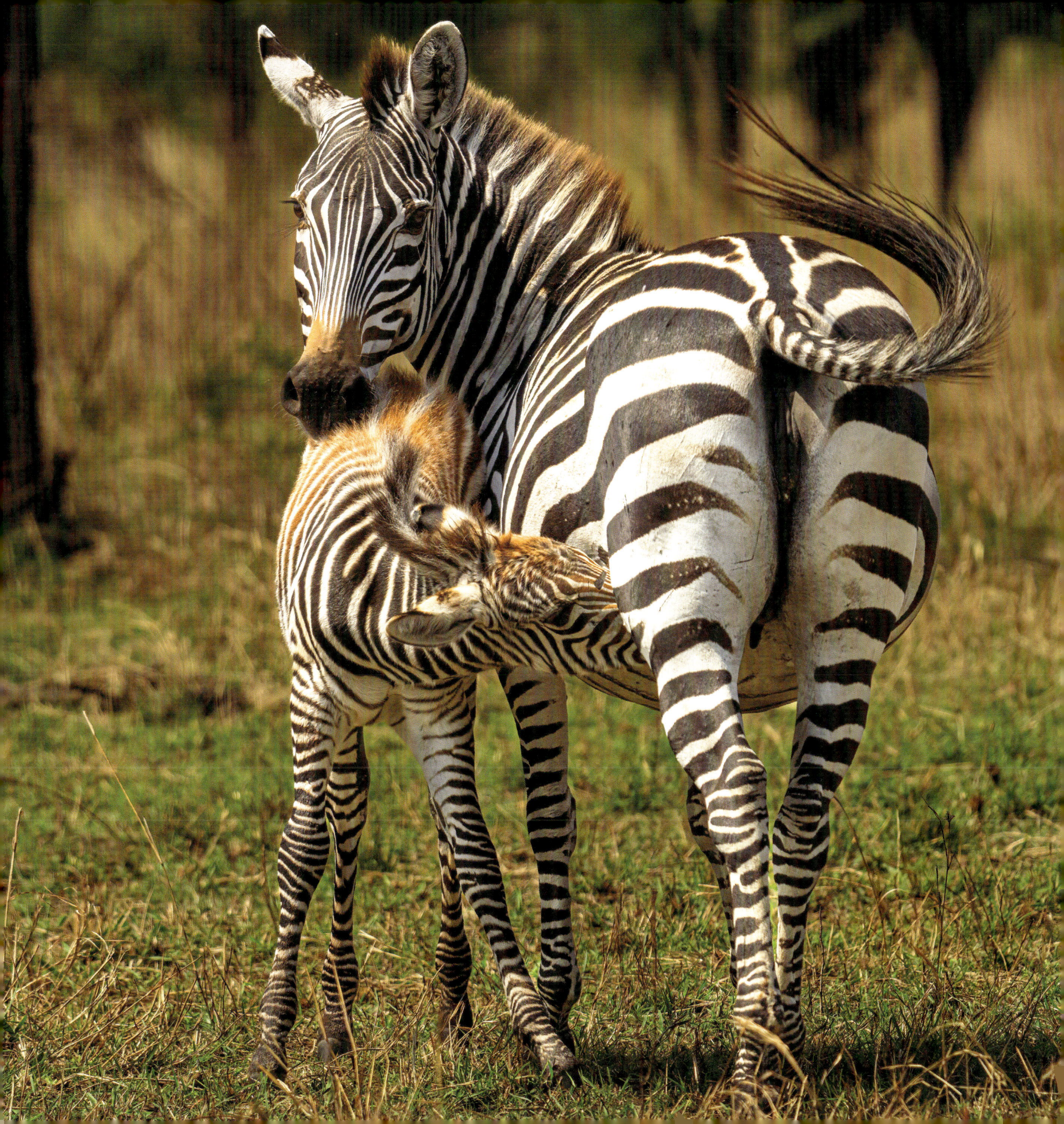

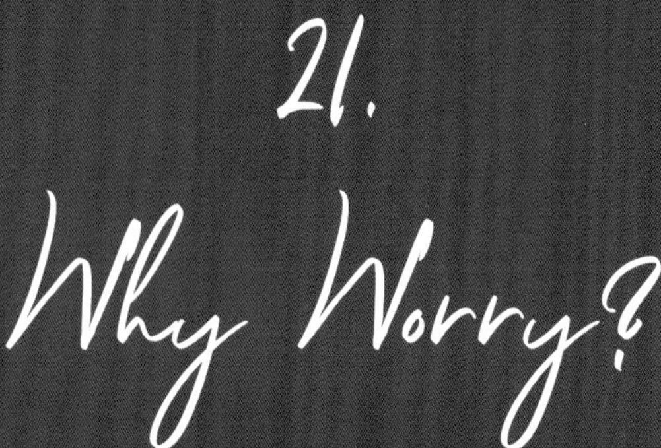

21. Why Worry?

This osprey was perched above the river preparing to dive when, out of the blue, a kestrel swooped in like a bullet at 60 miles an hour. The stunned look on the osprey's face tells the whole story.

Long ago, I learned that most of the bad things I feared never happened. I also learned that often there was not much I could do to prevent the bad things that did happen. In both cases, I decided that worrying was a complete waste of time.

You will live and die whether you worry over it or not. In the final analysis, the best course is to enjoy every day of your life without losing sleep worrying. When the storms come, as they inevitably do, deal with them and move on.

This kestrel's attack on the osprey wasn't just a harmless annoyance. While kestrels are much smaller than other hawks and ospreys, they can be just as lethal. They disable their prey by striking with their bill at the base of the neck to injure or separate the nerves in the spinal cord or use their talons to rake across the back and neck of birds in flight. Either injury can be fatal.

Jesus said, "Don't worry about tomorrow, for tomorrow will bring its own worries. Today's trouble is enough for today." Matthew 6:34 (NLT)

A few moments after this surprise attack, you'd never know the osprey could have lost its life. Today, this osprey survived the kestrel's attack. One day, that may not be the case. Meanwhile, he didn't waste time worrying, but went back to the task God created and designed him for. He promptly returned to fishing.

To excel at wildlife photography, you must develop the ability to focus entirely on your subject. It is important to intently watch the subject, alert to its every movement, ready to respond, without overthinking the details.

BOISE RIVER, IDAHO | ISO 1600 | 441MM | 1/2000

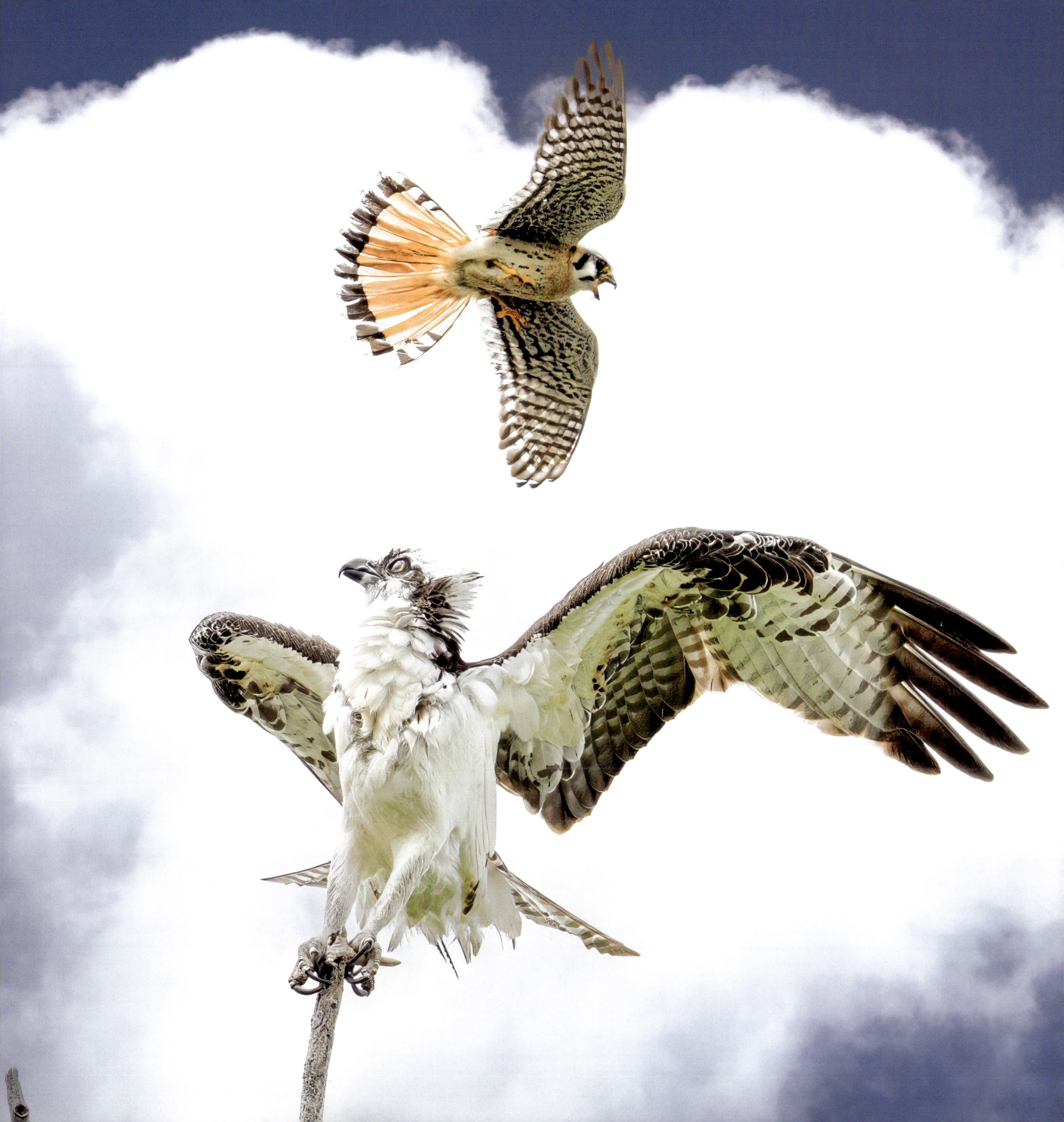

22.

Sisters

Our Masai guide told us that this family of lions is actually two sisters and their cubs. Unlike male lions, the lionesses in a pride have no rivalries. They will hunt together and fiercely defend each other and the cubs for their entire lives.

My wife has one sister. Maureen and Corinne are and always have been inseparable. Not that they haven't squabbled—Corinne says Maureen used to chase her around the house with a broom. Maureen counters that she was justified because Corinne refused to help with the chores. Corinne insists she did her share of other jobs.

I don't know which version is true. In almost 40 years, I haven't seen either of them sit down for long. Both keep constantly busy caring for their families. I have also never heard either one raise her voice, let alone argue with the other. Both Maureen and her sister are industrious, hardworking, and quick to lend a helping hand. From the treasure of their hearts, these two gracious women pour their love into friends, family, and all who cross their paths.

A lion pride includes up to a dozen lionesses and almost all of them are related. Male lions come and go but lionesses are the pride's hunters and defenders. Just like these lionesses, Maureen and Corinne see to every need of their families, and when necessary, they are their first line of defense.

While my wife and her sister share many admirable qualities of other more dainty species, there is no question that Maureen and Corinne are the lionesses of our family.

The lions were drinking from a stream below my vantage point. Including the incline as a blurred foreground draws the viewer in while eye contact and the lioness's readiness to spring lends dynamic tension to the composition.

SERENGETI NP, TANZANIA | ISO 2000 | 295MM | 1/1000

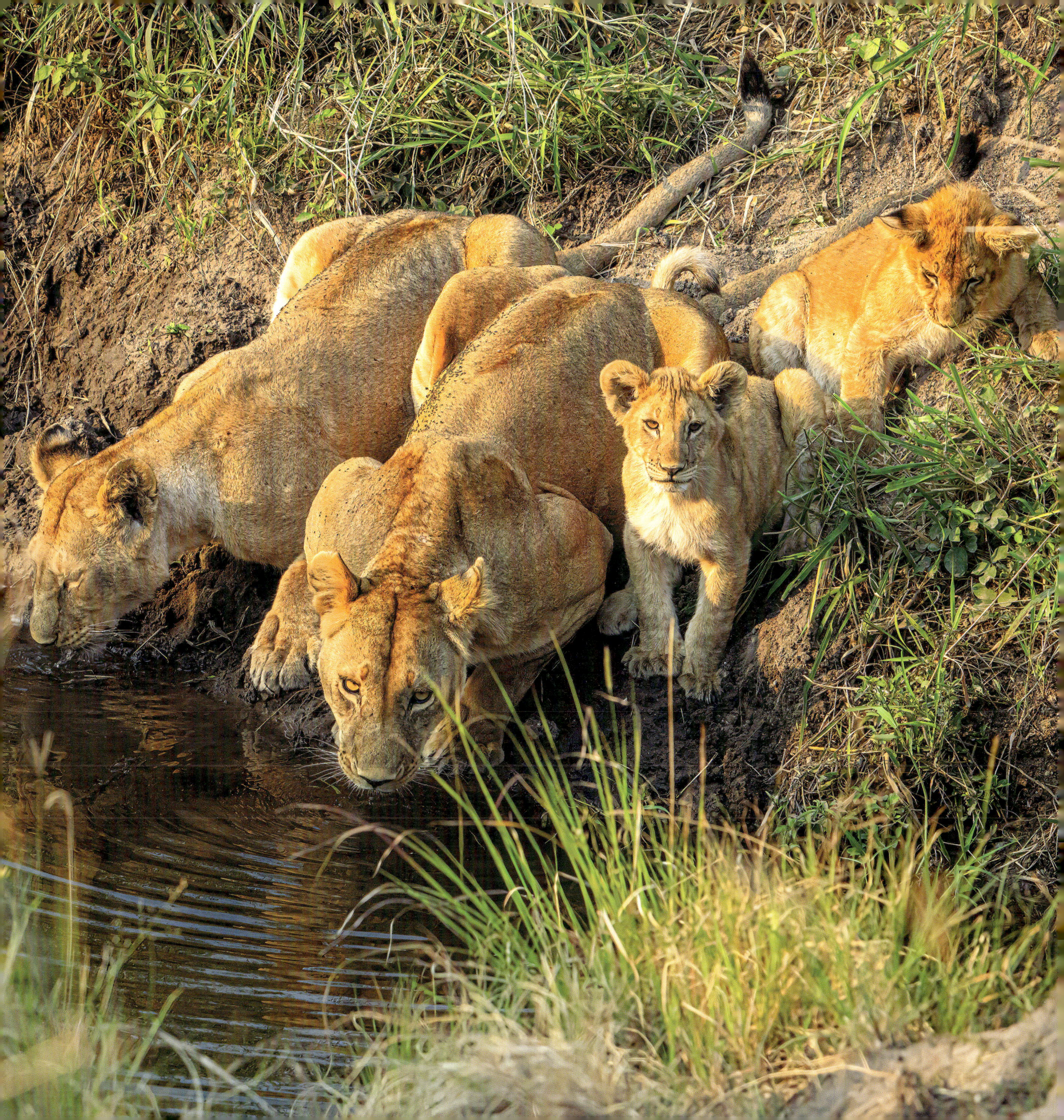

23.

Bette Davis Eyes

This cuddly little lemur is as gregarious as a monkey. Found only in Madagascar and neighboring islands in the Indian Ocean, this rare, wet-nosed primate lives in trees and feeds on bamboo, fruits, insects, and small animals. The lemur is active at night, which explains its striking eyes. The lemur's cornea has reflective tissue that seems to glow in the dark. Its eye colors vary from iridescent yellow to green and orange. Not menacing like the lion or tiger, not piercing like the eagle or osprey, instead, these eyes are translucent, mesmerizing, deep pools of light—a little bit like Bette Davis's eyes.

When Bette Davis arrived by train to Hollywood, the studio representative left her at the station because he couldn't find anyone who looked like a movie star. But her depth and intensity on screen were mesmerizing. And then there were "the eyes."

Bette Davis's eyes were blue but appeared hazel in black and white film, not burnt orange like this lemur. With giant pupils bulging from her eye sockets, her eyes seemed in shock or filled with righteous indignation. I remember her scaring the daylights out of me in *Whatever Happened to Baby Jane?* and *Hush . . . Hush, Sweet Charlotte*.

Bette Davis's eyes were famous long before Kim Carnes sang these lyrics:

> *She'll tease you, She'll unease you, All the better just to please you*
> *She's precocious and she knows, Just what it takes to make a pro blush*
> *All the boys think she's a spy, She's got Bette Davis Eyes.*

> *Direct eye contact from the subject is incredibly powerful. When eyes are prominent in a photograph, you are immediately drawn to them. This is one of two photographs not taken of an animal in the wild.*

ONTARIO, CANADA | ISO 1000 | 480MM | 1/80

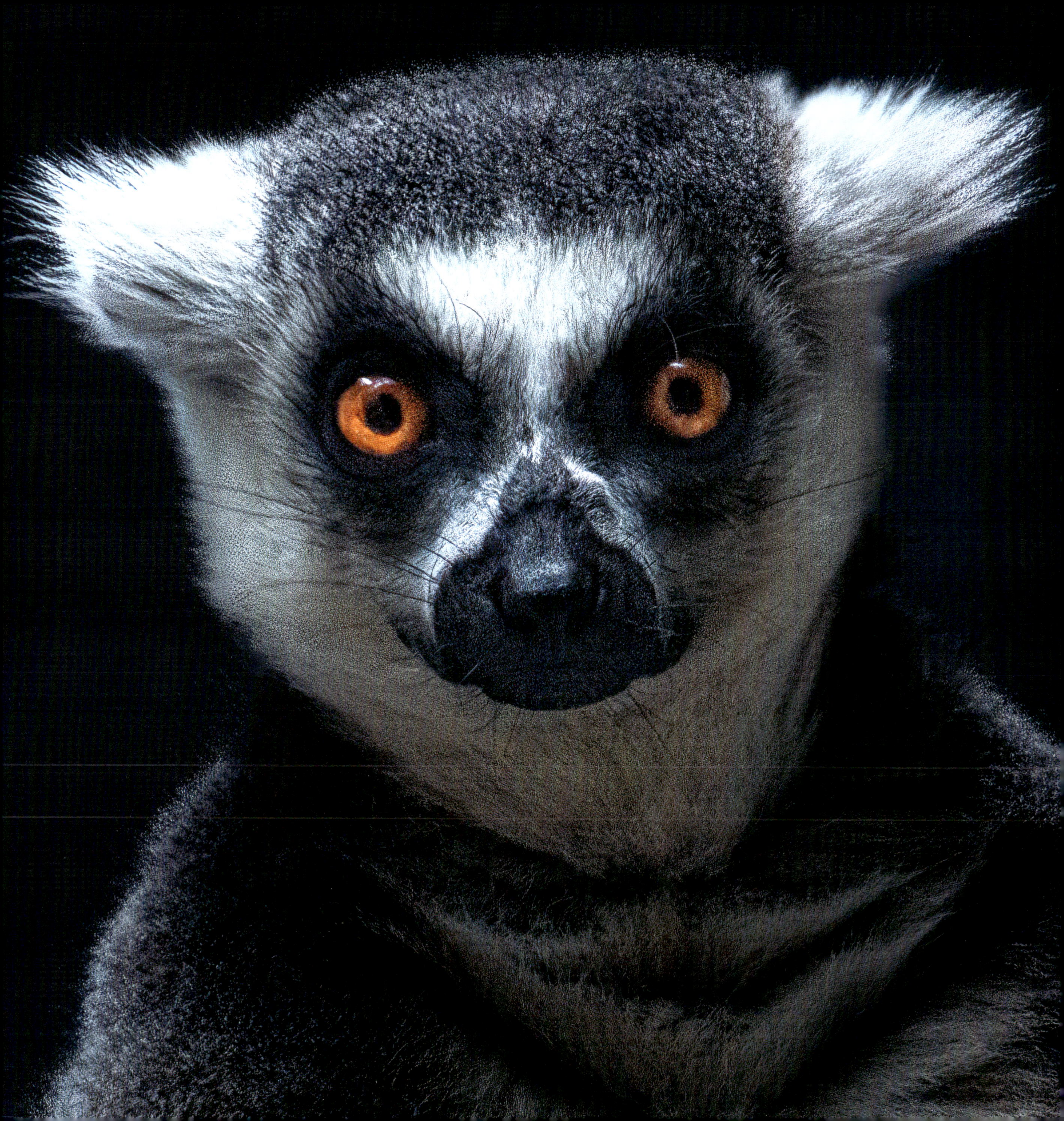

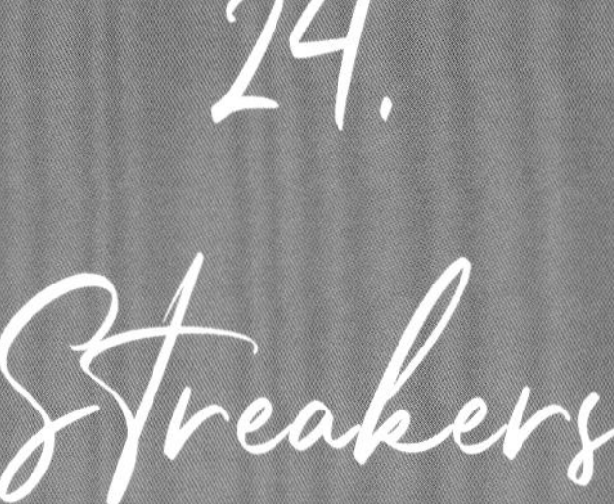

24. Streakers

These are young wild turkey chicks, or "poults," from which we get the term poultry. At this age they have very few feathers; so to me they look like little streakers.

We had a bath ritual when I was young. After dinner, Mom herded all us kids into the bathroom adjacent to the kitchen, where she told us to remove our clothes and step into the big claw-footed tub already filled with warm water and bubble bath. Four of us—my brother, myself, and two of our sisters—unceremoniously stripped down and plopped into the soapy water, splashing until there was more water on the floor than left in the tub.

Mom would soon intervene to stop our fun. One by one, she lifted us out of the tub and toweled us dry. We were ordered to walk to the bedroom, towel-clad, to change into pj's.

Like that was going to happen. Instead, as each of us was set free, we burst through the kitchen, through the screen door, and out onto the sidewalk, where we ran up and down in our birthday suits, snapping our towels in the air and shouting raucously to all the neighbors sitting on their front porch swings up and down the street.

Apparently, we and the poults had something in common.

Ah, the innocence and joys of childhood!

I chose a focal point at the bottom of the frame with a shallow depth of field to direct the viewer's attention to the front of this troop and accentuate their hasty march.

BOISE RIVER GREENBELT, IDAHO | ISO 1000 | 600MM | 1/3200

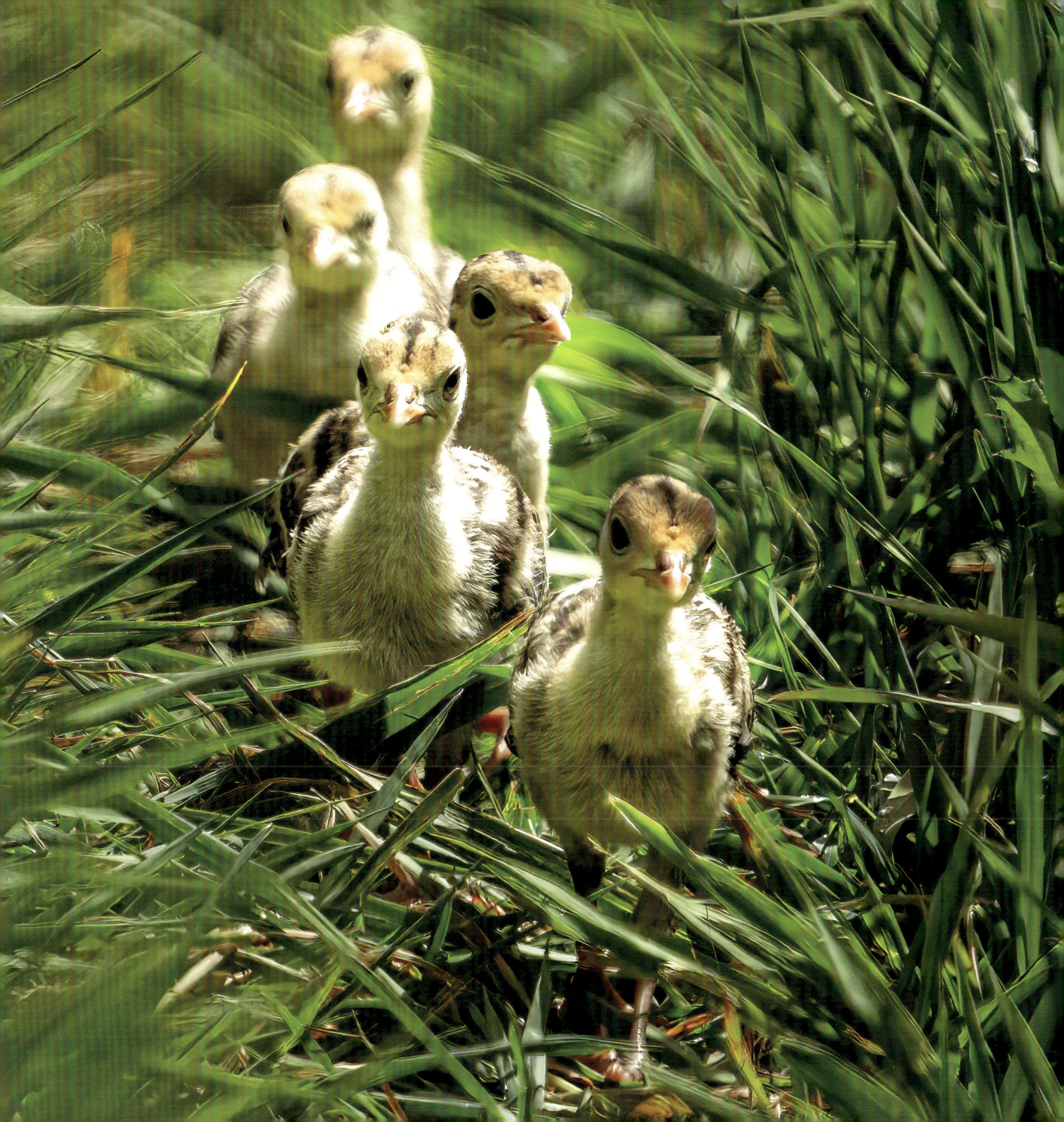

25.

Being Away

As our first day on safari drew to a close, we watched the sun set on giraffes peacefully munching leaves of acacia trees. Our guide turned off the engine of our Range Rover. All was quiet as time stood still. When we drove away from this spot, we felt refreshed, our minds filled with the tranquil beauty of the scene.

The scientific name for that experience is called "being away." According to a study by psychologists Stephen and Rachel Kaplan, it consists of two parts: First, a distraction from the worries and cares of the world. Second, an activity that involves "soft fascination," which means your attention is held without any effort. We looked on these giraffes and the sunset without needing to work at it or focus on anything in particular. We just soaked it in.

The Kaplan study found that being away yields tangible health benefits. First, your mind clears. Your thoughts, worries, and anxieties simply fade away. Second, you recover from mental fatigue acquired through the stresses of the day. Third, the gentle distraction, coupled with engagement in a low-stimulation activity, allows your mind and body to relax.

Enjoying nature as a regular habit will help you live longer and enjoy life more every day. When you come home exhausted and spent, consider a quiet nature walk. It's good for what ails you.

Placing these giraffes in their surroundings tells a story that a close-up wouldn't reveal. The soft lighting and serene surroundings convey a sense of peace and tranquility that a photo of the subject alone would miss.

AMBOSELI NP, KENYA | ISO 3200 | 200MM | 1/1000

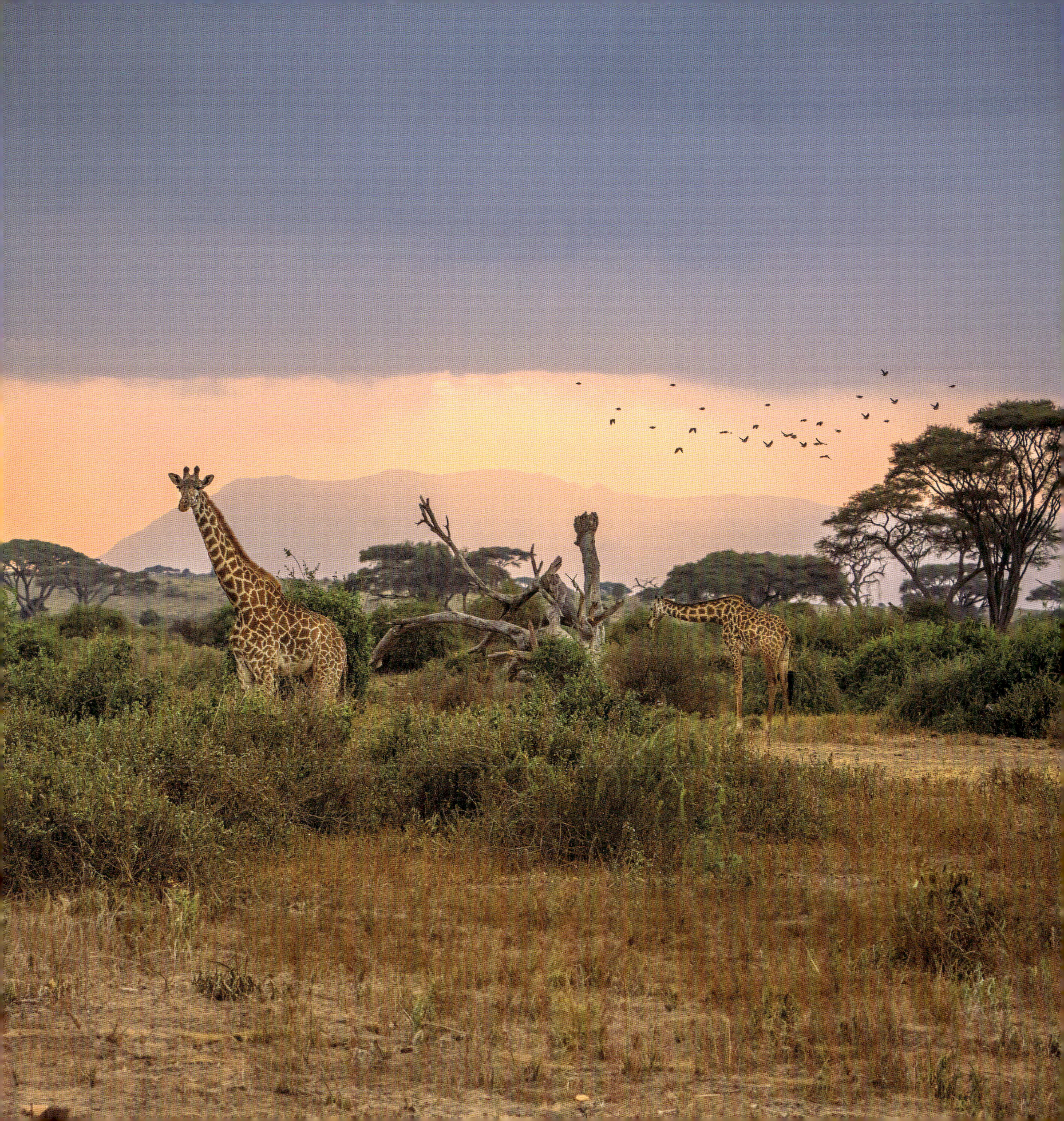

26.

Light at the End of the Tunnel

This tunnel is on a road running through Hells Canyon, the deepest river gorge in America. It could be a metaphor for the state of the world, trapped in a dark tunnel of loneliness, fear, anger, depression, and for some, hopelessness. But there is always a light at the end of the tunnel. Somewhere, a flower blooms, a bird sings her beautiful song, and the sun shines brightly.

Scripture tells us, "'For I know the plans I have for you,' declares the Lord, 'plans to prosper you and not to harm you, plans to give you hope and a future.'" Jeremiah 29:11 (NIV)

On both sides of the tunnel, canyon walls climb out of the shadows almost 8,000 feet. There, perched high up on the mountain, live mountain goats. The one I photographed lives his life on rocky, treacherous slopes where the slightest misstep can bring instant death. But he is at home and at ease.

While his slim body enables this mountain goat to traverse narrow paths and lean close to the cliff walls, his hooves and pads are the key to his ability to thrive in this hostile environment. The feet of a mountain goat have soft pads that provide sure footing on the sheer cliffs, their hooves are split so they can spread and provide more stability, and their back legs have dew claws to stop a downhill slide.

We too can have a sure foundation for protection from the storms of life. Jesus said, "Everyone who hears these words of mine and does them will be like a wise man who built his house on the rock. And the rain fell, and the floods came, and the winds blew and beat on the house, but it did not fall, because it had been founded on the rock." Matthew 7:24-25 (ESV)

I photographed the tunnel as a frame to contrast its darkness with the light beyond and the off-white mountain goat among black rocks, looking down to convey the light above overcoming the dark. A photo's composition tells a story.

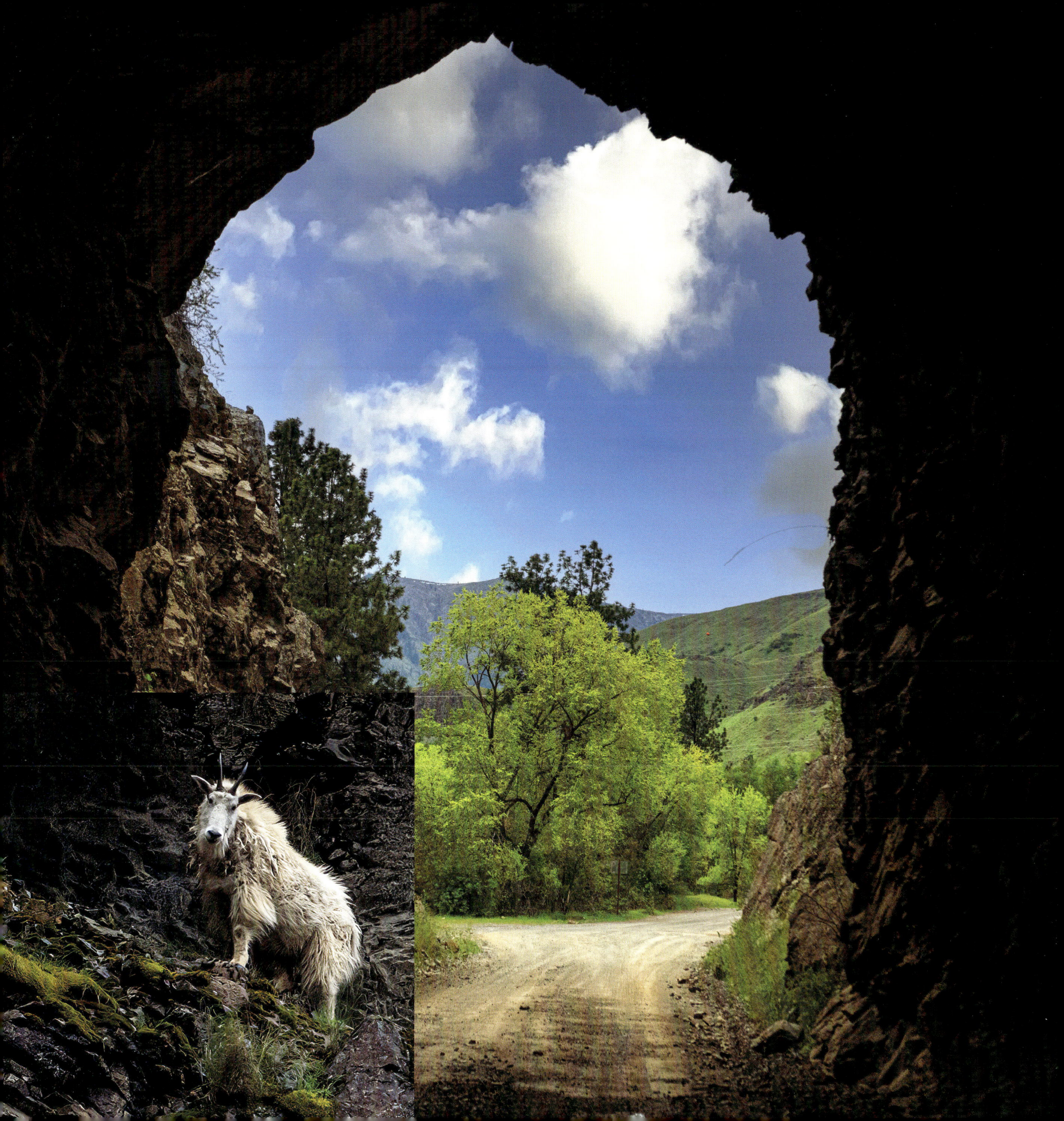

27.

Hearing Is Seeing

This statuesque impala is the most elegant of the antelope species. There are 74 species and 56 subspecies of antelope in Africa.

The species of antelope are incredibly varied; each one is beautiful in its own unique way. The waterbuck has long-ringed horns and a nose shaped like a heart framed in white, while the tiny klipspringer resembles a little elf-like animal. It is called the "goat of the rocks." Then there is the impala, with graceful lyre-shaped horns; sleek, reddish-brown and white coat; and incredible speed. Those qualities and its "dancing on the grass" behaviors make it by far the most fun to watch.

Notwithstanding the impala's beauty and grace, because of their speed, natives refer to them as "McDonald's antelopes," because they are fast food for cheetahs.

Just as every picture tells a story, every story paints a picture. Everyone has a life story. Each person is as unique and lovely as each of these many types of antelopes. I hope I get to photograph all the antelopes, and I hope I get to hear many more life stories. I love hearing them. It's been a wonderful part of my life.

If you are like me, you only need to see one beautiful sunrise like this one to want to hear more stories.

The sun's low angle and its soft golden light when this photo was taken create slight shadows and expose the fine detail in the coat of the impala, while the narrow depth of field blurs the background, creating separation from the subject.

SERENGETI NP, TANZANIA | ISO 500 | 356MM | 1/160

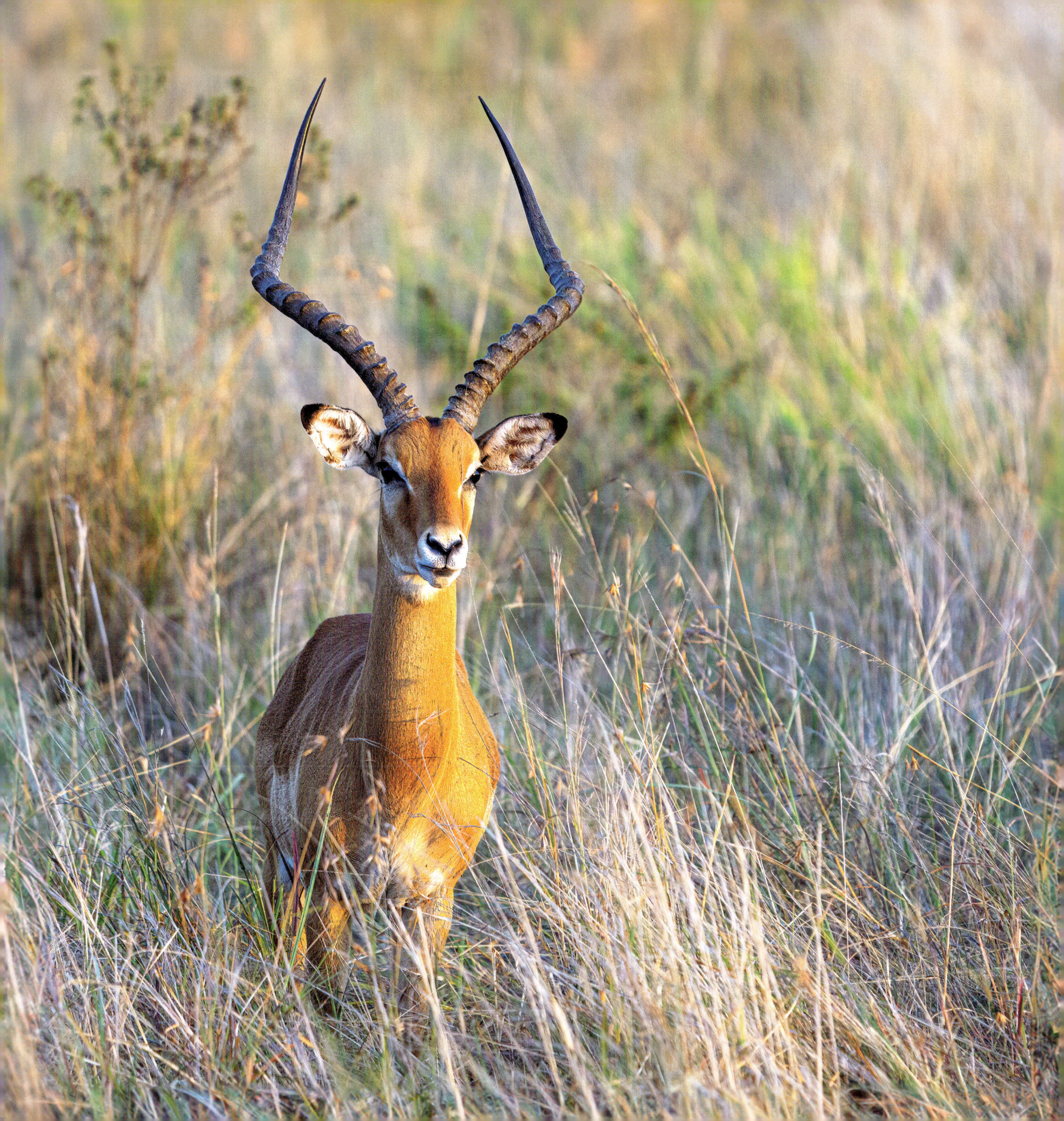

28.

Time for Lunch

This photo shows guppies desperately trying to elude the huge bill and pouch of a male brown pelican, the smallest species of pelican worldwide. That pouch can hold up to three gallons of water and fish. Watching this pelican down hundreds of little guppies with apparent relish and delight reminded me of my own experience with these tiny fish.

On a visit to a small Caribbean island, I was invited to a local church potluck. I was hesitant to experiment with foods I couldn't recognize. So I was pleased to see some tasty-looking corn cakes and helped myself.

At first bite, I realized something was off. Then I glanced at the crescent hole left from the bite I had taken, and a mass of sightless little guppy eyes stared back at me. Needless to say, lunch for me was over.

You may be far more gastronomically adventurous than me; if so, I wish you happy guppy-guzzling. As they say in Rome, "De gustibus non disputandum est," which translates to, "There is no accounting for taste."

I went to Florida for two days to photograph ospreys, but they only showed up one of the days. Rather than call it quits on the other day, I went looking for other interesting wildlife and was rewarded with this lovely pelican.

SEBASTIAN INLET SP, FLORIDA | ISO 1000 | 459MM | 1/2500

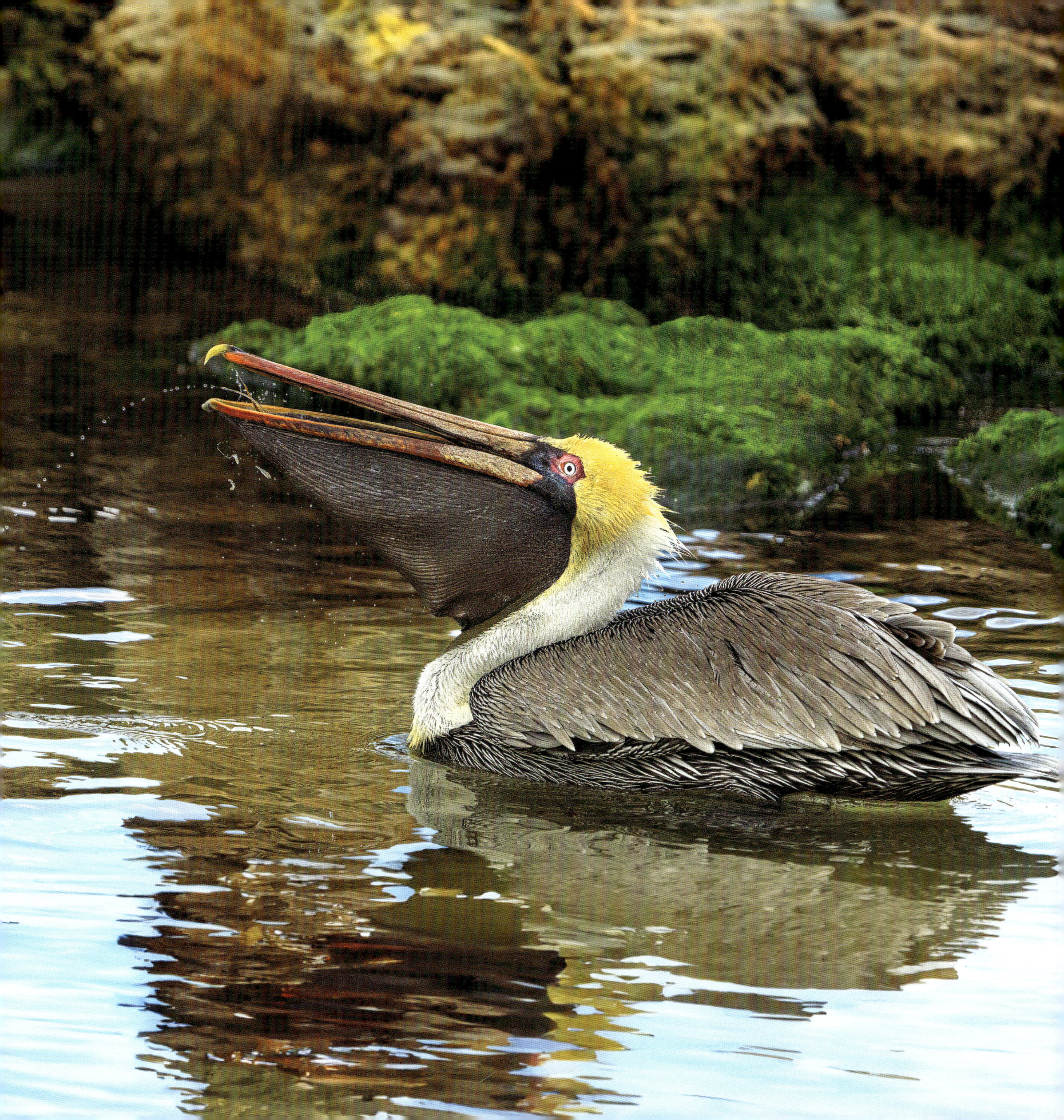

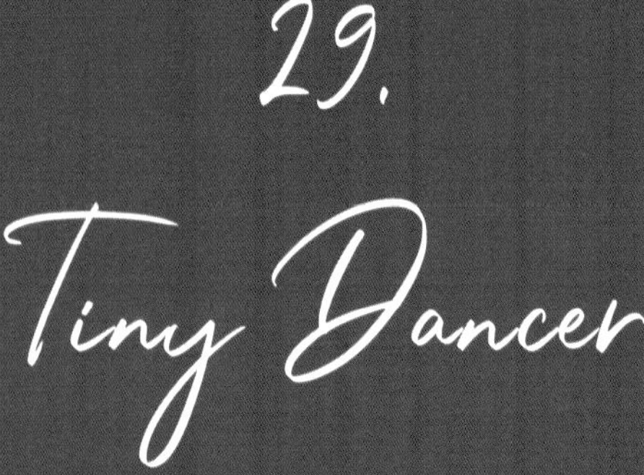

This miniature ballerina of a bird is a snowy egret. It is actually a small heron. The word “egret” comes from the French “aigrette” (little heron). The snowy egret was almost wiped out in the 1800s by hunters who slaughtered them for their white feathers, which were the rage for bonnets and hair accessories. Today, however, they are protected and flourishing.

John James Audubon was an early 19th-century French artist, self-taught ornithologist, and naturalist. *Birds of North America*, his life’s work, contains his 435 life-sized drawings of North American birds. He spent a great deal of time studying and painting the snowy egret. Its larger cousin, the great egret, is the emblem for the *Audubon Society*.

Because their yellow feet contrast so vividly against their white bodies, Audubon said, “They appear to dance in the shallows on golden slippers.”

This brilliant white snowy egret pops out of the dull background because the background is blurred. To get that result, I opened up the aperture as wide as the light and my camera lens would allow.

SEBASTIAN INLET SP, FLORIDA | ISO 1000 | 600MM | 1/3200

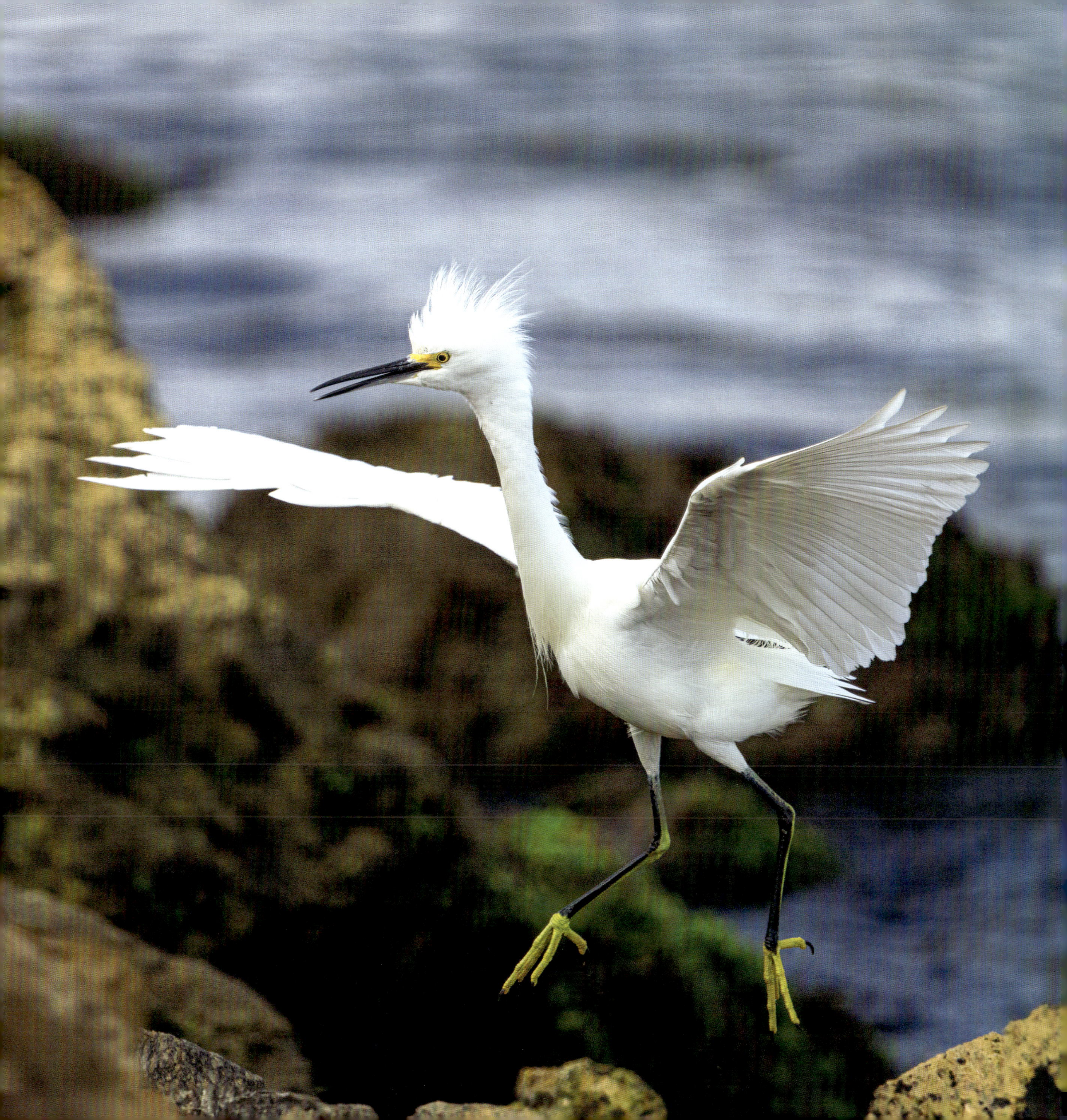

As we sat at a "bush breakfast," this parade of elephants ambled toward us. It was a spectacle.

Elephant herds are actually the extended family of one matriarch and her offspring. The matriarch makes the decisions, leads the herd to food and water, provides for their defense, and nurtures their young.

This herd's approach brought to mind other giants who have walked into my life.

Proverbs 16:19 (NLT) says, "We can make our plans, but the Lord determines our steps." Everything happens for a reason.

As a law student, I applied to work as an intern with a law firm. George Catlin took me under his wing. Every day he bought my lunch—with a catch. We ate at the Church of the Open Door, listening to a Bible study and talking about life. George showed me I could be a Christian and a lawyer. It changed my life.

God brought other giants into my life as well. In my first challenging case, Bruce Jagger became my mentor. Bruce was the archetype of the great lawyers of history; brilliant, unflappable, a soul of wisdom. When my life was falling apart, I met Pastor Bob Pruett, who remained my friend through difficult years and taught me the most important life lesson—that God's love is sufficient. Steve Crane, my current pastor, with wisdom beyond his years, has become my new role model. In each of these great men, humility, integrity, and love overflow. Although Bob and George have passed, what they taught me is with me forever. Giants have undoubtedly walked into your life as well.

After an elegant breakfast in the bush—with white tablecloth service, including champagne—we began our first full day of safari in Kenya and were greeted by this herd of elephants calmly walking toward us in a procession.

AMBOSELI NP, KENYA | ISO 1000 | 303MM | 1/1000

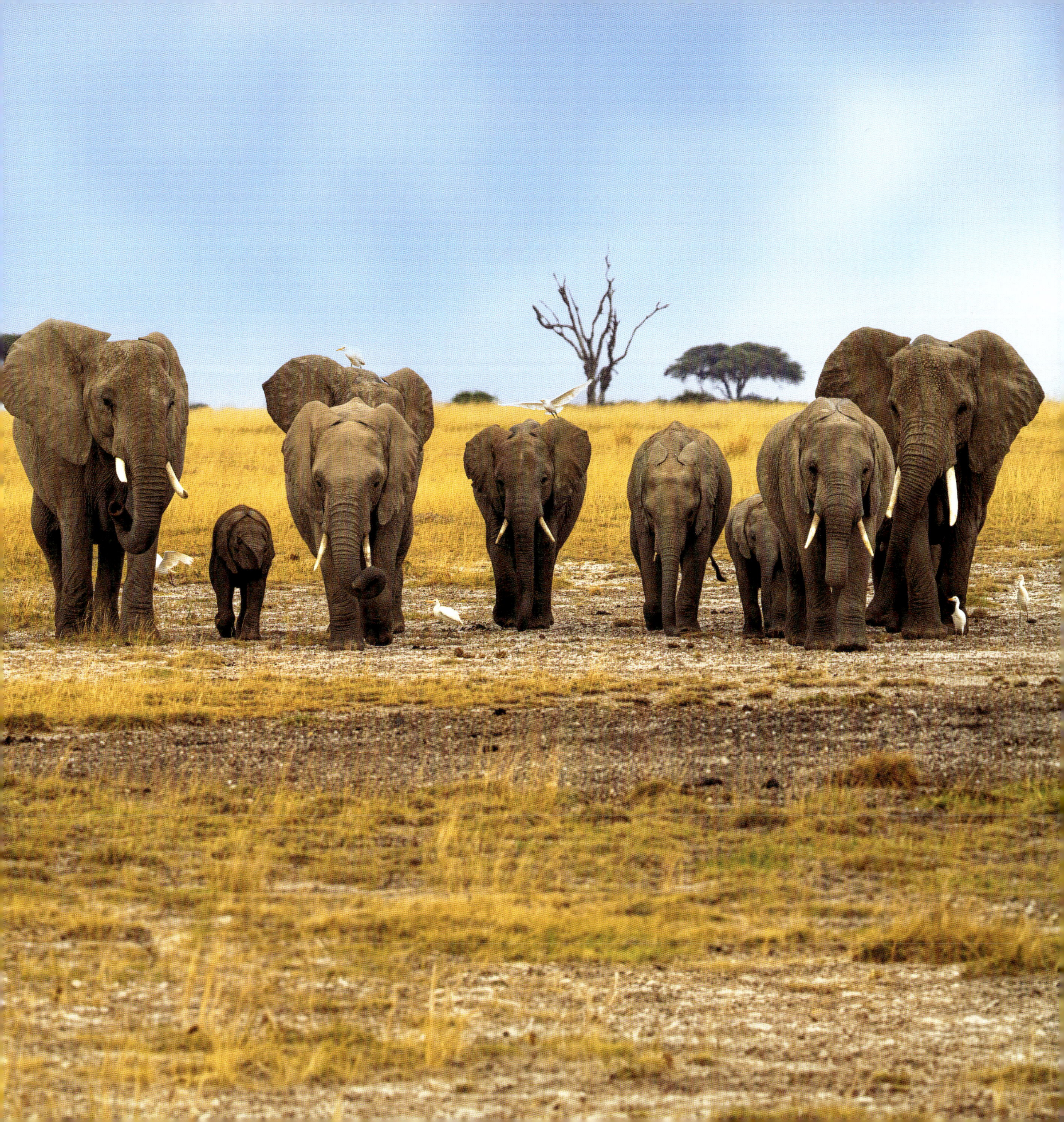

31.

Miraculous

Until 2005, scientists couldn't explain how the bumblebee could fly. Its stubby body and short wings would seem to make flight impossible. The bumblebee clearly did not get that memo. With the aid of high-speed macro photography, biology professor Michael Dickinson at the University of Washington solved the mystery.

If a bumblebee's wings moved up and down, they couldn't possibly generate enough downward air pressure for the bee to fly. But they don't. Instead, their wings move back and forth and tilt downward on forward movement and upward on backward movement, like a helicopter. The tilt angle shifts with perfect precision on each forward or backward swing, enabling what vaguely resembles a C-130 Hercules to fly effortlessly on the slightest of diaphanous wings. All this happens so fast it creates an almost hurricane force around the bee that propels it through the air. The wings of the bumblebee move with such blazing speed that it takes a shutter speed of 1/4000 of a second to freeze them.

With the mystery of flight resolved, it now appears that the impossible has given way to what can only be described as the miraculous.

Focusing on small, fast bugs like this bumblebee in flight can be a challenge, but most good cameras provide a zone- or area-focus feature that finds the moving object if you get it anywhere in your viewfinder. It works best with an open sky.

BOISE, IDAHO | ISO 1250 | 105MM | 1/4000

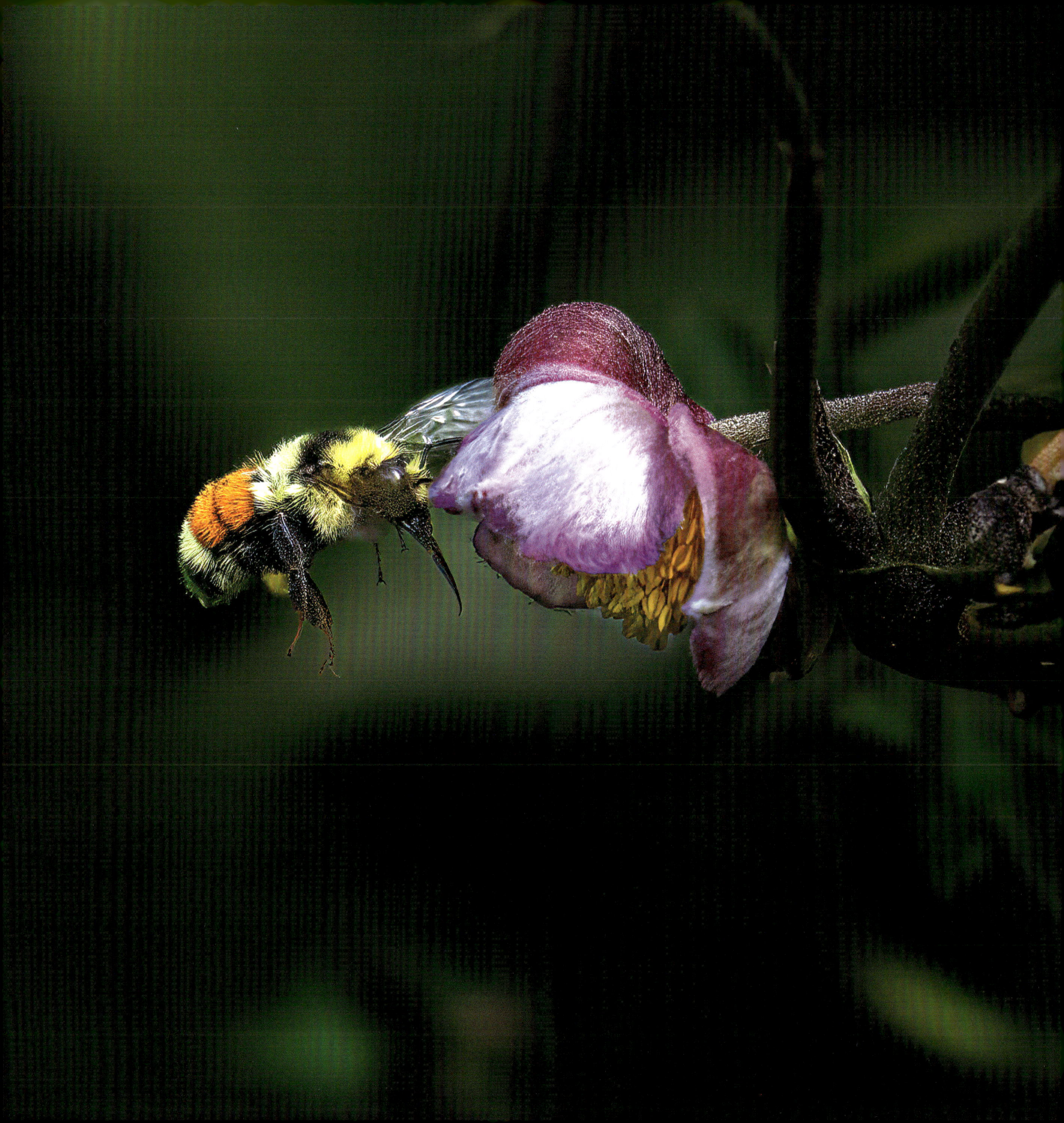

32.

Soaring

I saw this eagle on a cloudy day soaring across a bay in Puget Sound. It was a magnificent sight. The eagle seems to have a command of the skies, effortlessly soaring in the clouds.

Whenever I see the sweep of an eagle's wings as it gracefully takes to the air, a sense of awe wells up within me. There is a regal majesty and strength in the eyes and wings of an eagle.

When the Declaration of Independence was signed on July 4, 1776, John Adams, Thomas Jefferson, and Ben Franklin were asked to design a seal for our new nation. The story that Franklin wanted the turkey instead of the eagle for our nation's seal comes from a letter he wrote much later to his daughter, Sarah. In that letter, Franklin criticized the eagle, calling it "a bird of bad moral character" that "does not get his living honestly," but steals fish from other birds, while he thought the turkey was America's "original native" and a "bird of courage."

While I respect the turkey, which is beautiful in its own right, I am glad we chose the eagle. Just think how awkward Thanksgiving dinners would be if the turkey were our national emblem. I wouldn't know whether to say grace or sing "The Star-Spangled Banner."

Absent the levity, though, when I see a bald eagle flying high over my head, it brings to mind the words of Isaiah:

"But those who trust in the Lord will find new strength. They will soar high on wings like eagles." Isaiah 40:31 (NLT)

This eagle was photographed at a considerable distance from the shore in Puget Sound. I set my camera for continuous autofocus so that once I had the bird in focus, the camera would track it and constantly refocus.

SILVERDALE, WASHINGTON | ISO 800 | 500MM | 1/2500

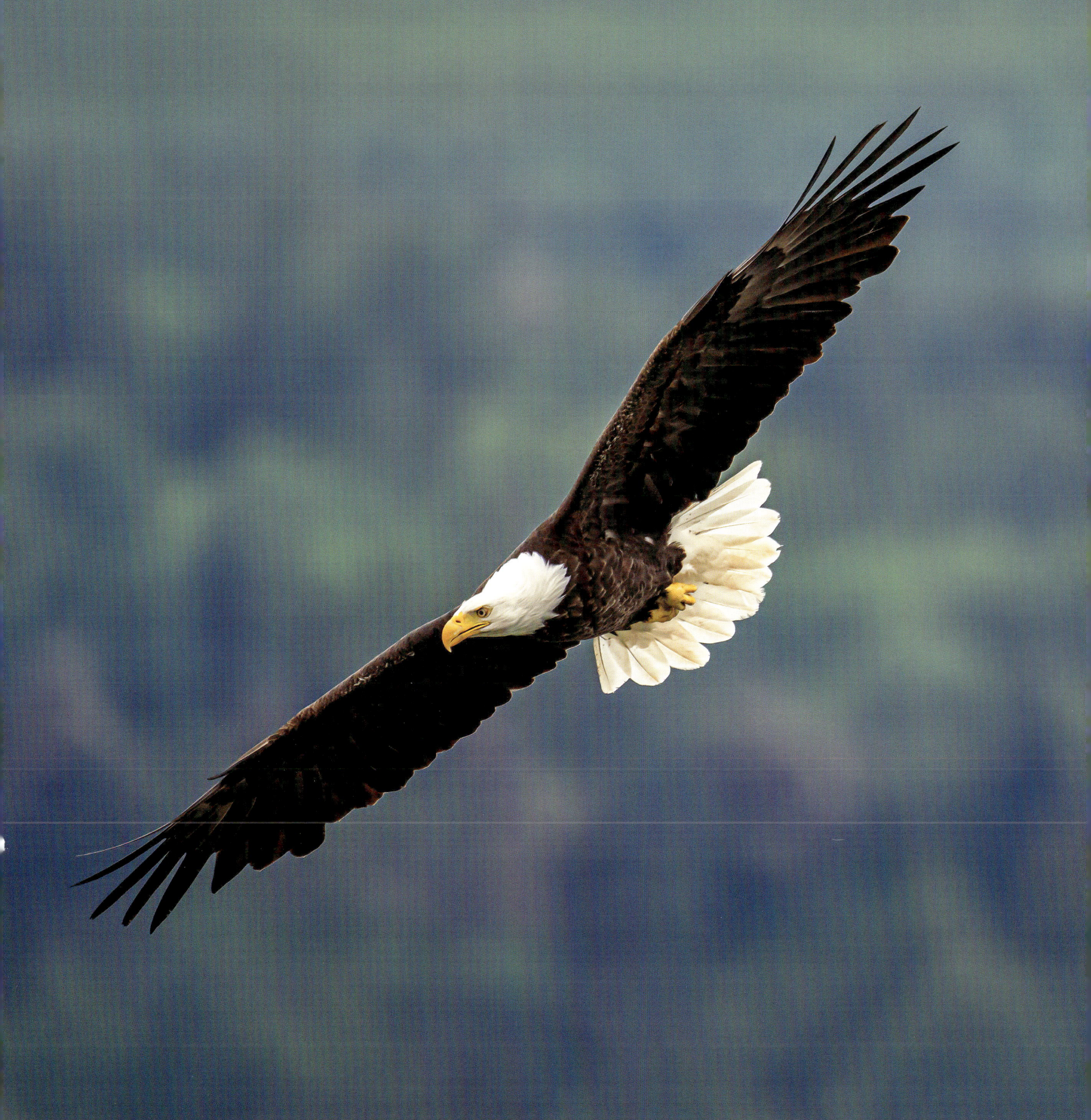

33.

At the Lake

I snapped this photo of the sunset on a fishing trip to the Northwoods.

When we were young, our parents rented a $35/week cabin in Wisconsin. Not much of a vacation for Mom, but us kids had a ball fishing, swimming, hunting for salamanders and crayfish, and roasting hot dogs and marshmallows.

One summer in the nearby town of Hayward, we watched a lumberjack festival with tree climbing, wood chopping, and log rolling on the Namekagon River. I also saw my first drive-in movie, *Operation Petticoat*, with Cary Grant and Tony Curtis. Dad loaded us into the station wagon in pajamas. Mom brought a huge bucket of popcorn and Coca-Cola. They put a blanket on top of the car and we sat on the roof, ate popcorn, and watched the drive-in movie about a pink submarine.

On the way home Dad gave us the "roller coaster" experience, hitting the gas on inclines, then lifting his foot when he reached the top. Our stomachs churned, and we screamed in delight.

When I grew up, I asked Dad how he was able to take so much time in the summers for these family trips. He told me, "The office wasn't making much money anyway, so it didn't cost me anything to close it down for a few weeks."

Summers at the lake were magical, and I will carry memories of campfires and sunsets in the Northwoods for a lifetime.

The brilliant colors in this sunset are true to life, but if I had taken this photo on auto mode, my camera would have washed them out. I set the white balance manually and fooled the camera into adding warmth to the photo.

OGOKI RESERVOIR, ONTARIO, CANADA | ISO 125 | 26MM | 1/250

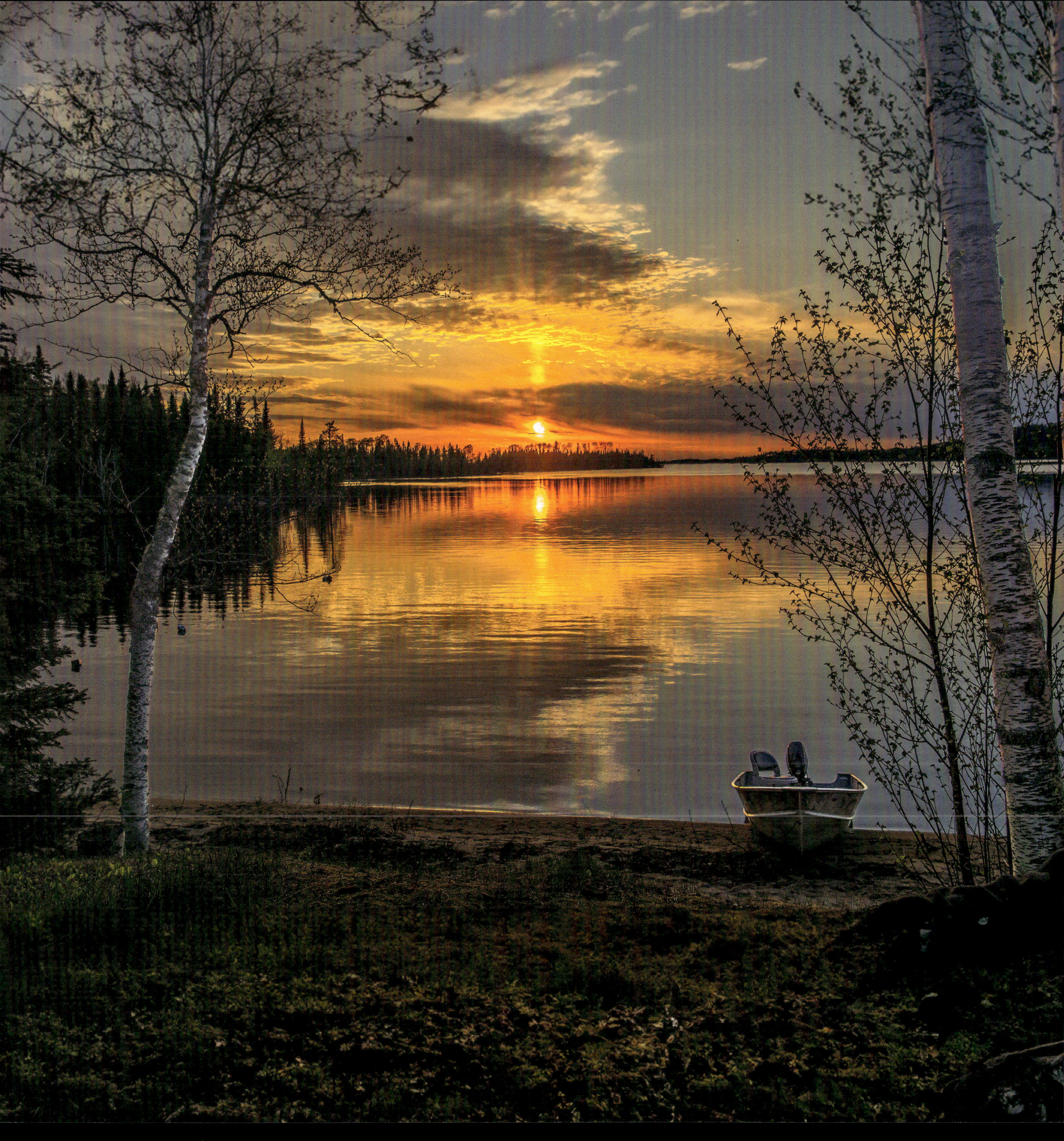

34.

Seeing on Purpose

When you are in your backyard or at a park, you might have caught a glimpse of a dragonfly, but I bet you don't remember it. Your attention was elsewhere. You didn't really see it.

To really see a dragonfly, you have to look for them on purpose. That is a philosophy of life. Whether you look for dragonflies on purpose says a lot about how you live your life. I am trying to become a person who looks for dragonflies on purpose every day. Because nature around us is exquisitely complex and irrepressibly beautiful. And it shows off God's genius.

The English poet William Blake expressed it eloquently:

> *To see a world in a grain of sand*
> *And a heaven in a wild flower,*
> *Hold infinity in the palm of your hand*
> *And eternity in an hour.*

I am glad that I didn't miss seeing this dragonfly in the final stages of its short lifespan. Most of its life was lived underwater as a nymph, and only two months are spent as an adult dragonfly. Then it is quickly gone. There are many different kinds of dragonflies, and all are intricate and beautiful. When I took this photo, my attention was on the performance of a new lens on my camera, not on the presence of dragonflies. Imagine what I might have seen if I had been looking on purpose.

Dragonflies aren't very big, so I used a shallow depth of field to blur the background. Some blurs are blotchy while others are soft and creamy. We call the latter good "bokeh," and that is solely due to the optics of the camera lens.

BOISE, IDAHO | ISO 1600 | 600MM | 1/1600

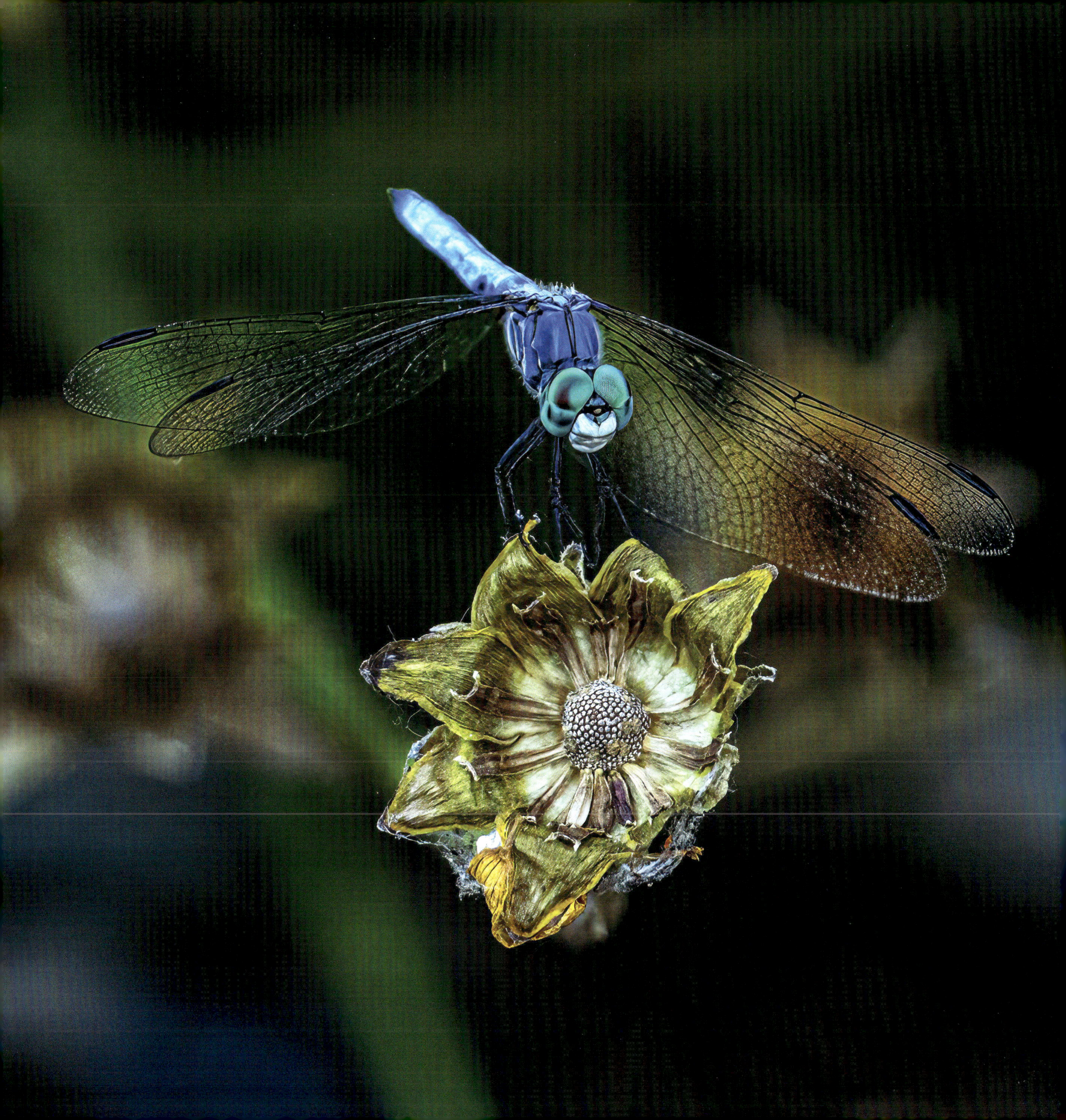

35.

Surreal

This is Esau, one of the last super tusker elephants in the world. Having satisfied my craving to photograph a super tusker up close while lying in the grass as he walked toward me, I now hoped to photograph Esau silhouetted in the setting sun with Mount Kilimanjaro as a backdrop. But clouds obscured the iconic mountain peak.

We followed him for close to an hour across the savannah, bouncing up and down ravines and mounds in the tall grasslands. He was the only large animal moving across the plains. Our object was to get the sunset over the mountains and behind Esau.

As the sun disappeared leaving a beautiful pastel sky behind this massive elephant, I took my last photos of Esau ambling south across the African plains—the real king of the beasts.

This photo is a combination of three images taken in a single burst. Each was set at a different exposure, one for the sky, one for the background, and one for the elephant. They were stacked into one photograph to bring out the beautiful colors in each part of this incredible setting.

The experience was quite surreal.

This photo was my first attempt at high dynamic range (HDR) photography. I took three photos in rapid sequence, exposing for the background, foreground, and my subject, and then stacked the three together to produce an image with deeper colors.

AMBOSELI NP, KENYA | ISO 6400 | 140MM | 1/6400

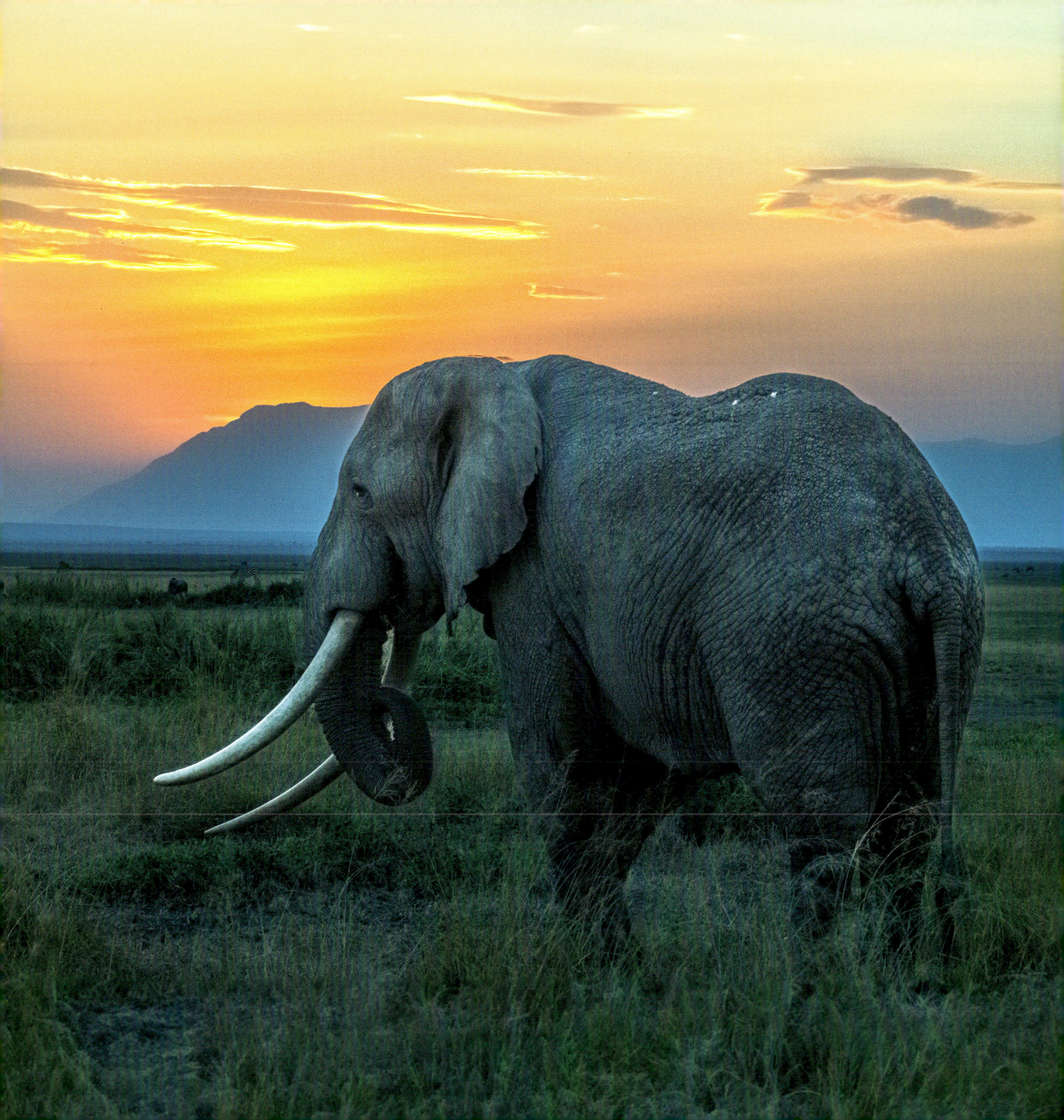

36.

The Fisherman

The ospreys' yellow eyes give them great color vision and allow them to see ultraviolet as well. They can see six to eight times farther than humans and can spot fish from up to 200 feet in the air.

Ospreys dive into the water head- and talons-first up to a meter in depth to catch fish, bending their wings at the elbow to provide the strength and mobility to come up out of the water with the fish in tow. Ospreys have a reversible outer talon; when they dive, two talons face forward and two backwards to grasp the fish like a steam shovel. There are small barbs on the pads of their feet called "spicules," which act like Velcro to hold onto a slippery fish while flying. Ospreys fly with the grace of a ballerina and determination of a fighter pilot. While aloft, ospreys will shift fish to face forward for aerodynamic flight to the nest.

I am a fair-weather fisherman. I fish to be with my friends and family. Catching fish is just a bonus. Not so for the osprey. He must catch fish. His mate and offspring rely on him, and he is perfectly suited for the role. Misses do occur, but a mature adult generally brings home dinner sooner or later.

But the osprey must learn how to catch fish. It is not an innate skill. When fledglings leave the nest, they fly with their mother to Central and South America where they spend the next two years in waters abundant with fish. Once they have honed their skills in friendly waters, they return to seek a lifelong mate.

Good wildlife photographers plan their shots and know their subjects. I studied osprey behavior in my neighborhood to learn where and when they fished. Then I set up a blind on the river and waited patiently to get this shot.

BOISE RIVER, IDAHO | ISO 900 | 500MM | 1/3200

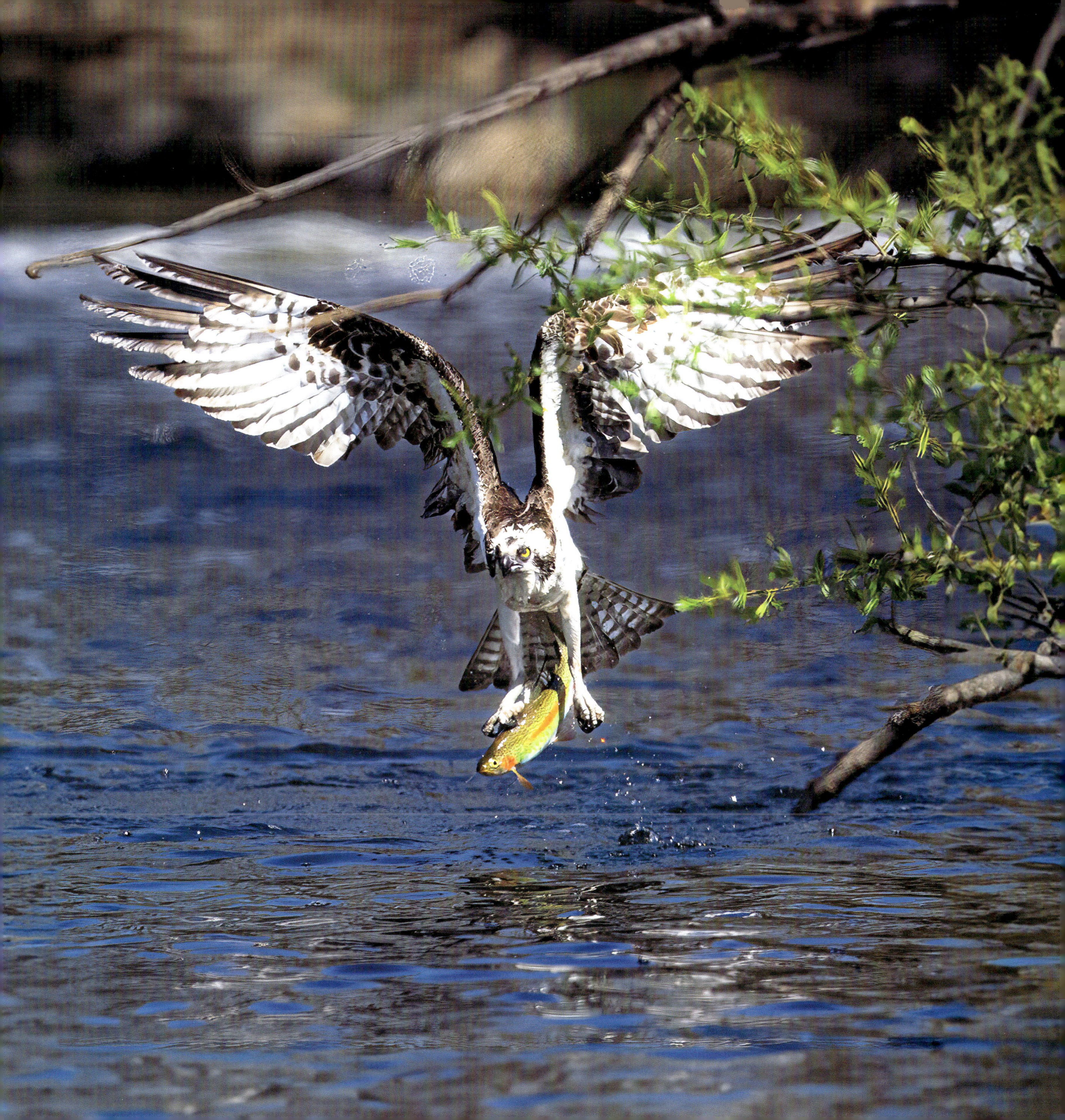

A smiling hippo like this one spends his days mostly submerged, hydrating and supporting his huge frame beneath the quiet waters of an African river. But looks can be deceiving. What lacks claws still has jaws!

Growing up we had a little dog who, like this hippo, was mostly belly. His name was Tony. He was adorable. Most days, little Tony peacefully basked in the cool grass of our front yard but secretly dreamed he was a big, bad guard dog.

One day, a policeman dropped by—not an unusual occurrence at our house since Dad was the town's mayor for eight years, then president of the Chamber of Commerce as well as a founder of the community college. It was a small town and no one was a stranger. Our weekly paper reported local events and a bit of gossip.

Tony greeted the lawman with tail wagging and rolled over, inviting a good belly rub. The policeman obliged and Tony struck, his jaws closing on the long arm of the law.

That was bad enough, but it got worse. The next day, the local headlines read, "Dog Bites Man as Man Puts Bite on Dog." The news spread like wildfire. Everyone roared. Everyone, that is, but Mom. She was mortified—and furious, especially since my journalism teacher wrote the story. Mom marched into the newspaper office and canceled our subscription that day.

Believe it or not, these "happy hippos" attack and kill more people than any other African beast.

Before I took this photo, I had no idea that a hippo's skin is so tough and leathery that it can stop a bullet or protect it from a crocodile's bite. I also didn't know they have hairy jaws.

MASAI MARA NP, KENYA | ISO 1250 | 359MM | 1/1600

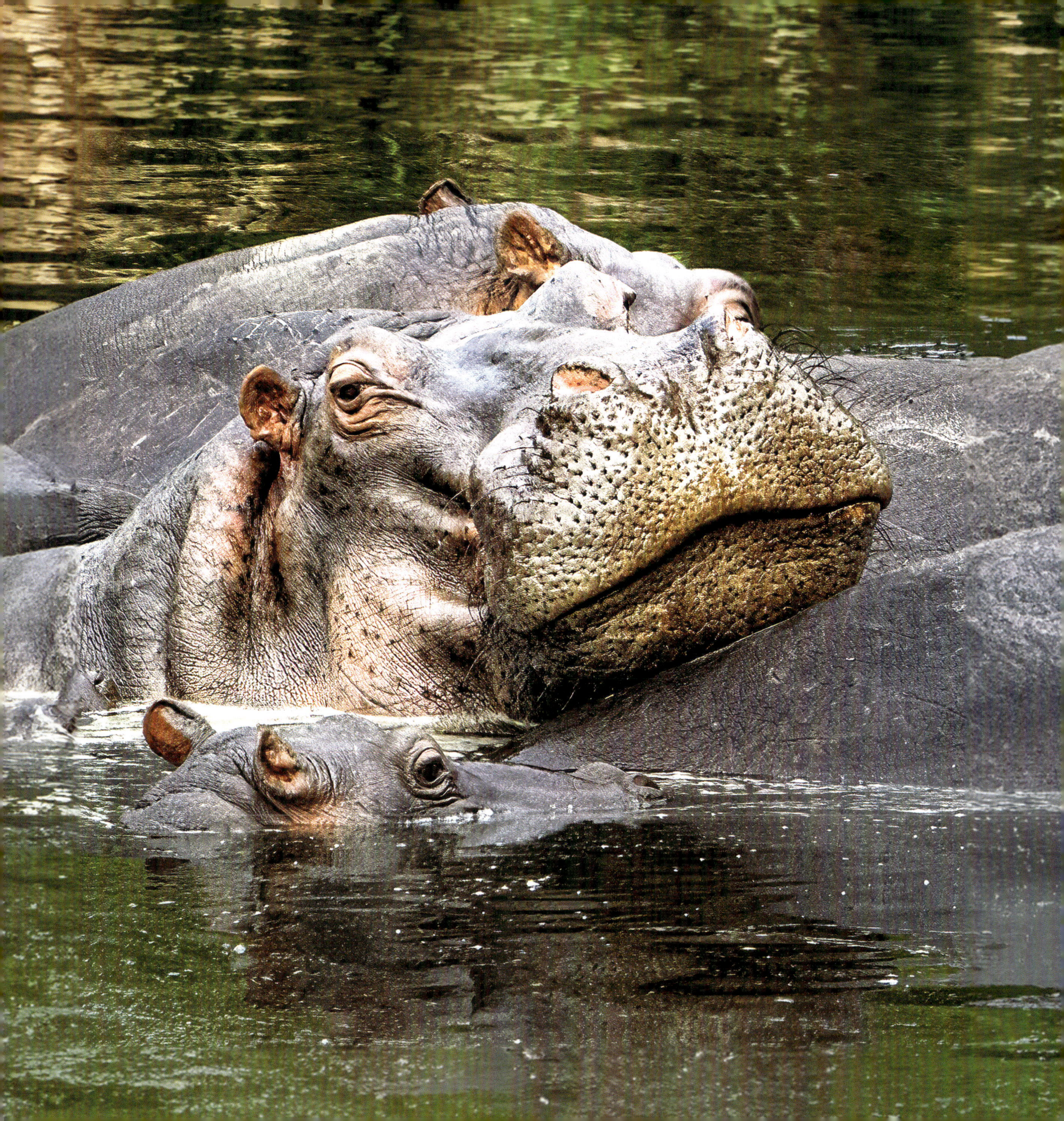

38.

If You Build It, She Will Come

"If you build it, she will come" is a way of life to the male African weaver bird. He builds the most intricate nests that hang from branches like a green Christmas tree ornament. He does so to attract a female. She may or may not choose to take up housekeeping with him depending on how attractive the nest looks.

When the male completes building his nest, he flutters his wings to invite females to his "open house." The discerning female selects her nest and her mate based on the appearance and convenience of the nest location. Wow! And I thought it was all about good looks and a nice personality.

Warning to the wise suitor—she's all about the nest.

On our safaris, we saw weaver birds outside almost every lodge. Since breakfast was typically on an open-air patio, they were a common sight, flitting with grasses or reeds in their mouths to their nests, suspended from tree branches.

HLUHLUWE, SOUTH AFRICA | ISO 3200 | 600MM | 1/3200

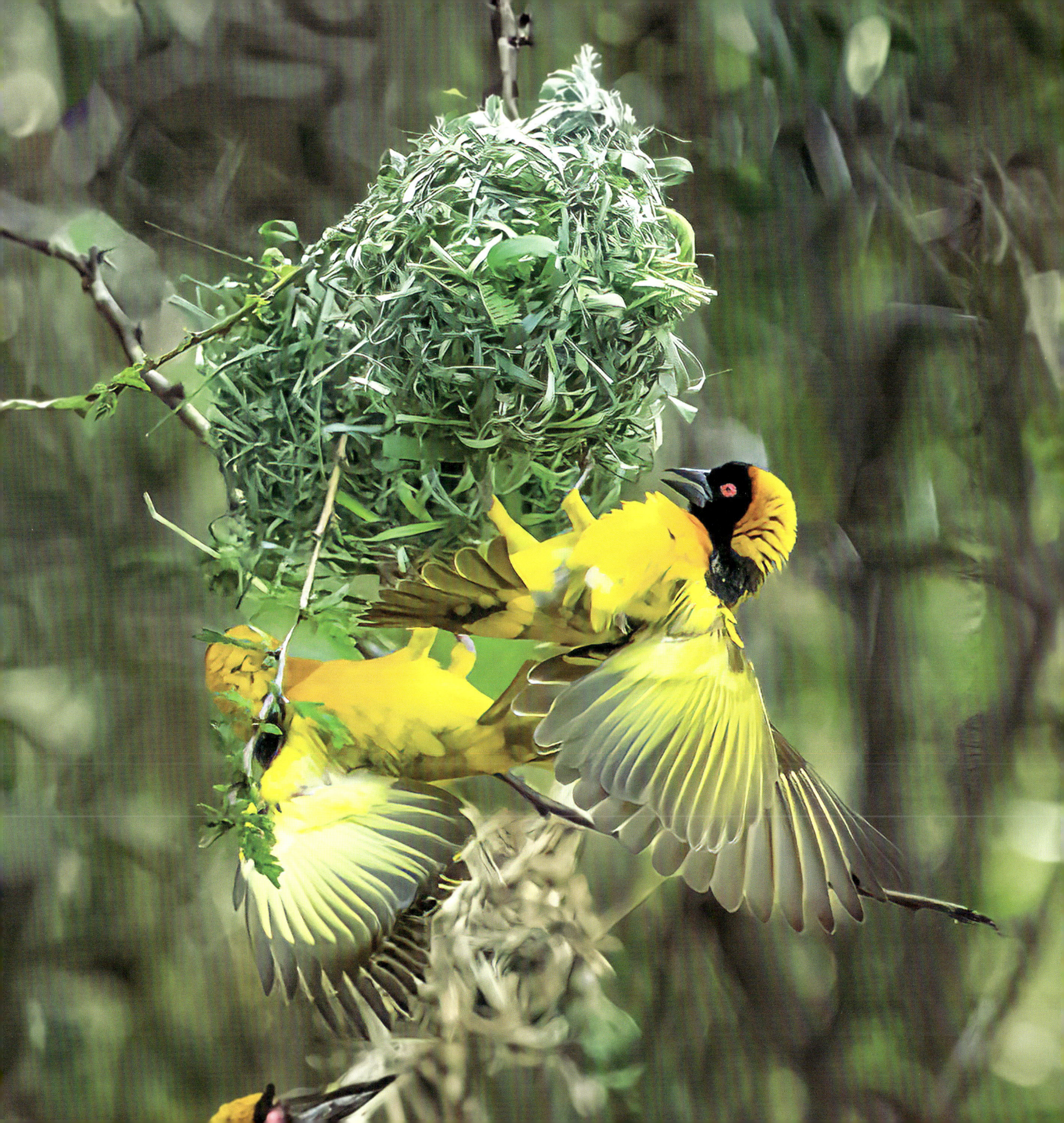

39.

Freeze-Frame

Ospreys are superb fishermen but don't always come home with their catch. These photos capture a pelican stealing an osprey's prize.

An osprey's aerobatic maneuvers are spectacular. When they catch a large fish, they need to balance it in flight. That may involve switching grips from one talon to the other and shifting the fish head-forward to cut wind resistance—all while banking and turning to avoid the assault of a larger airborne thief.

This entire aerial joust, from catch to chase to drop, took two seconds. Not nearly enough time for the naked eye to see or the brain to comprehend what just took place.

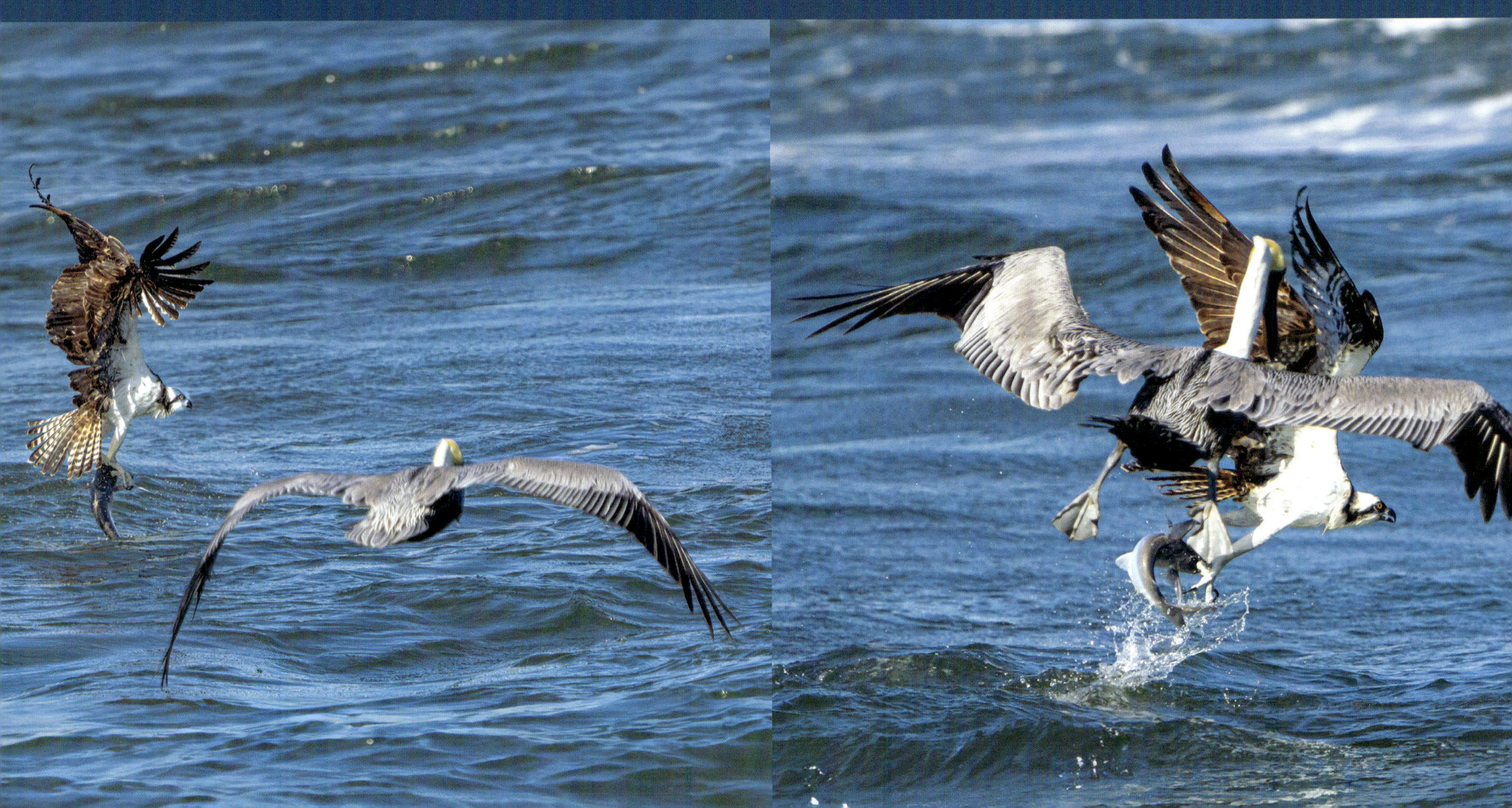

The camera has no such limitation. It can capture everything that occurs in a split second in exquisite detail. We can then revisit the action at our leisure and experience it in full. Frozen in time, the details emerge for the first time on full display. The significance of this is too often either overlooked or minimized.

Since I picked up a camera, the natural world has exploded in detail, color, texture, and motion. I took 10 photos of this encounter. All of them reveal the beauty of the osprey—in its eye, wings, legs, and talons. Perhaps the four included here will show you the value of freezing the moment and motivate you to pick up your camera.

> *To get this osprey-pelican series, I used a tripod. That allowed me to steadily pan horizontally with the birds as they flew across the bay. If I had tried this handheld, I doubt that I could have gotten these results.*

SEBASTIAN INLET SP, FLORIDA | ISO 500 | 600MM | 1/3200

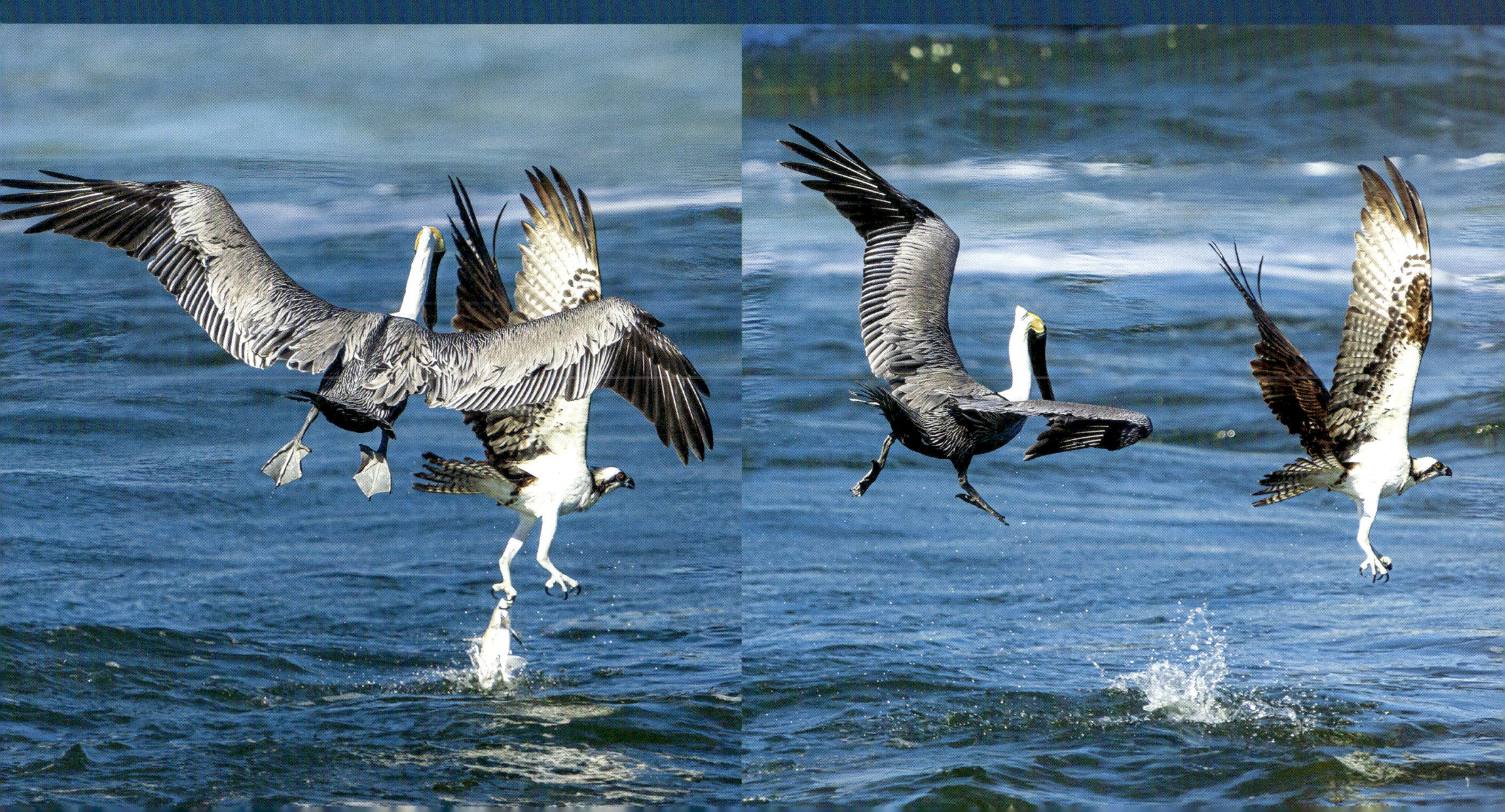

40.

In the Garden

Here are four of the many birds that live in our backyard garden, the Boise River Greenbelt: great horned owlet, California quail, kingfisher, and wood duck.

Our Boise River Greenbelt is the real treasure of the Treasure Valley. We live in a place where the beauty and majesty of God's creative genius is on our doorstep. In the middle of a metropolis, you can still find a quiet spot to sit on the banks of the river and hear songbirds sing, watch bald eagles and ospreys soar, great blue herons fish, and owls and hawks peer at you from a thicket or the branch of a tall cottonwood.

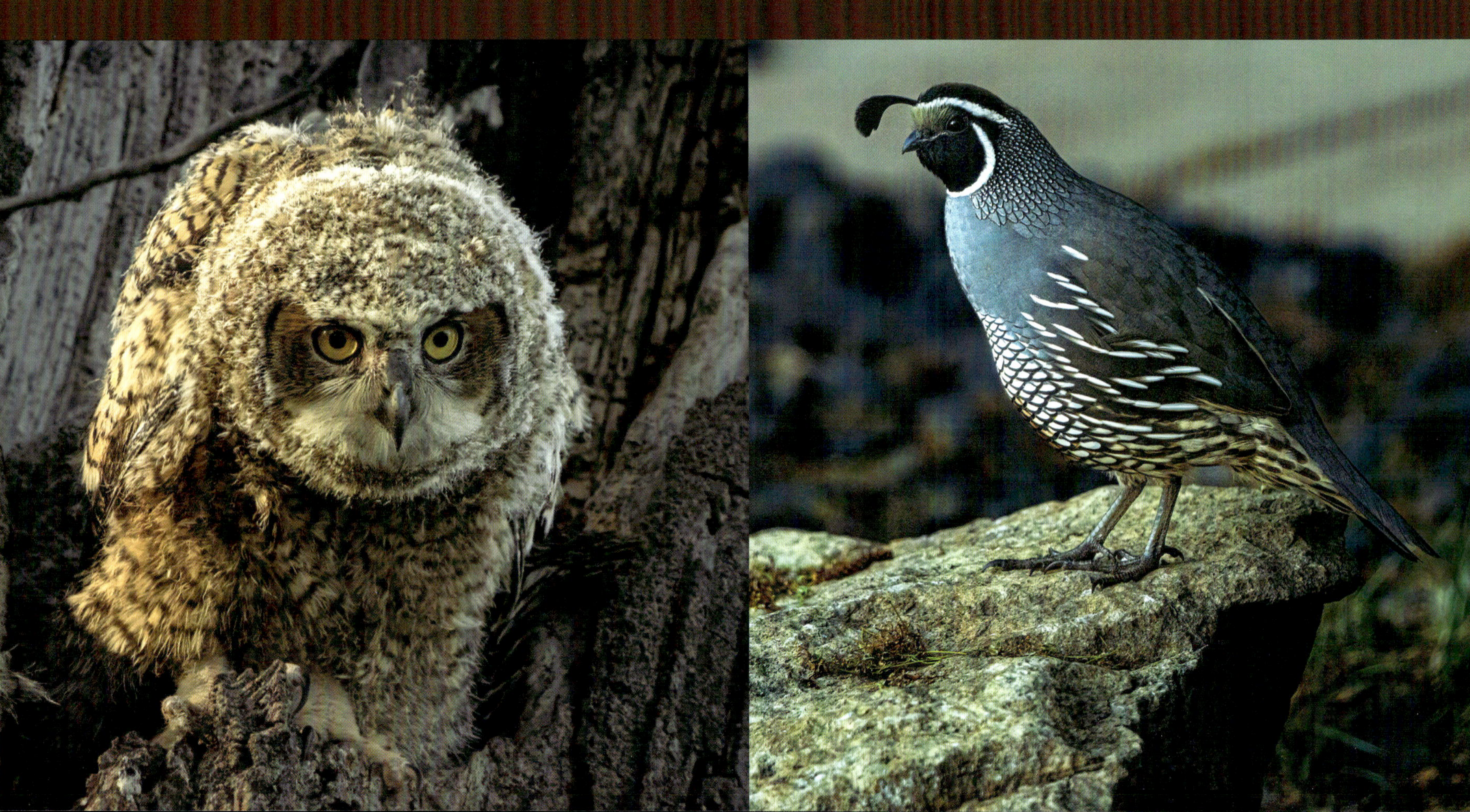

While many in my generation are still searching for a place where they can find peace, I am thankful to have found mine. The psalmist declares, “O Lord, what a variety of things you have made! In wisdom you have made them all. The earth is full of your creatures.” Psalm 104:24 (NLT)

All of these photos were taken on the Boise River Greenbelt a few minutes' walk from my home. I just went out to pick the low-hanging fruit. It's a good idea to dust off your camera and clear your head on a regular basis.

BOISE, IDAHO | ISO 1000 | 422MM | 1/500

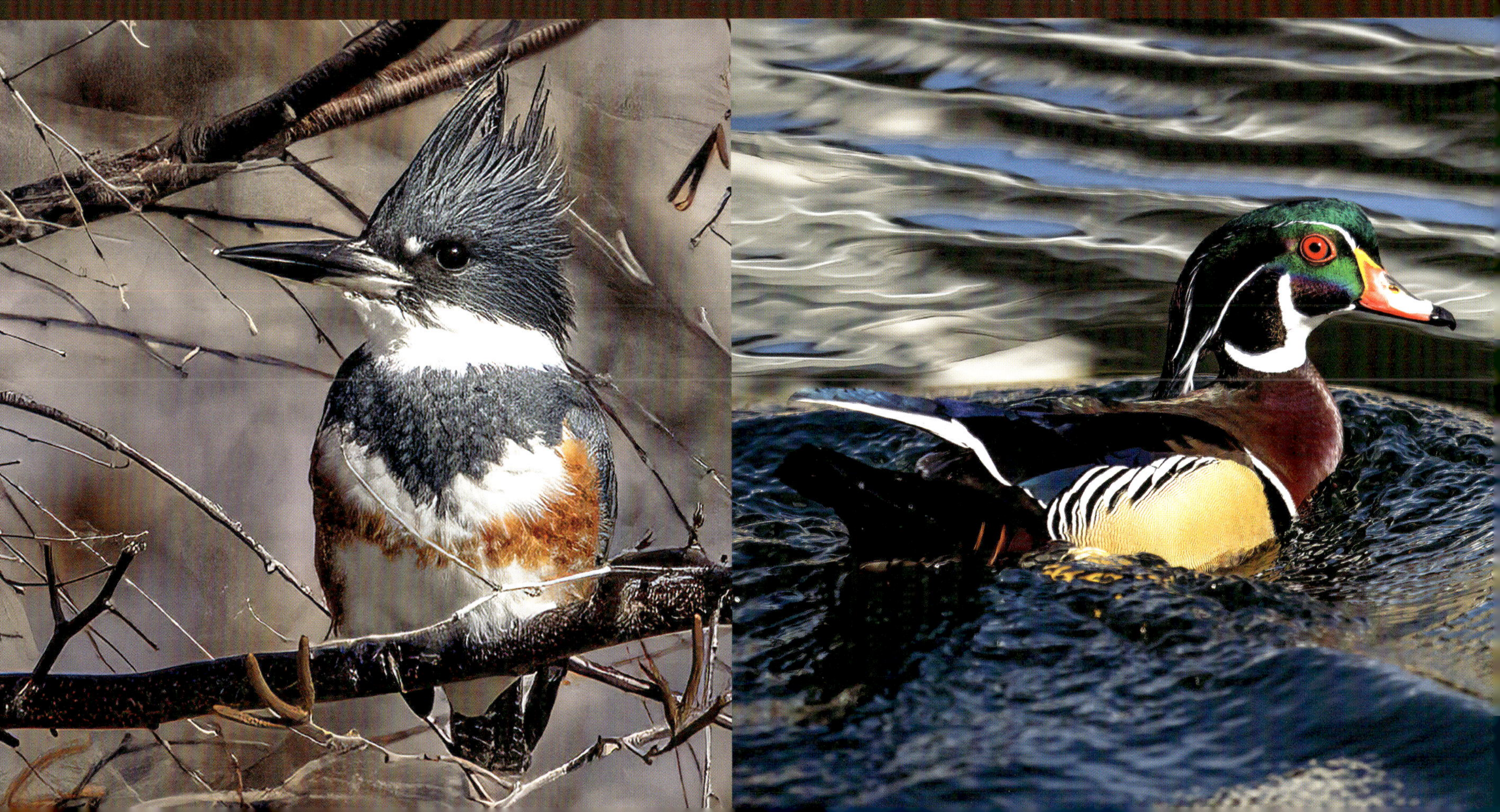

41.

Safari

Leopards, the most beautiful of the big cats, are nocturnal hunters, solitary and reclusive. They sleep most of the day high up in trees. As a result, they are difficult to find and photograph.

Leopards are powerful enough to kill animals as large as 1,200 pounds, although they typically target animals between 20 and 80 pounds. They routinely climb high up in trees carrying carcasses up to 100 pounds.

Maureen and I were on safari in northern Kenya. Up to this point, we were feeling safe. Apart from a couple elephants in Amboseli, we had no close encounters. Then our guide heard a leopard was spotted miles away. He drove at full speed up and down hills, over brush, and through several streams to get to it before it vanished. We were bounced all over the Range Rover. I was trying to hold on to two cameras and my seat. Maureen said she'd need to see a chiropractor after the trip.

Then we were there, not five feet from a gorgeous leopard, fresh off a kill. Unfortunately, the light was fading, though the oncoming dusk accentuated the mystery of this elusive feline. Because of the angle of the setting sun behind us, the blue eyes of the leopard appeared to have a purple cast.

Then the light failed us. We had to drive away—right into two massive female lions, hunting. Our guide stopped the vehicle and the lionesses walked on both sides, slowly, deliberately, not 10 feet away, while our vehicle was entirely open, with no windows. The lionesses were on the hunt—just thankfully, not for us.

Sometimes your camera can surprise you. The light was fading fast and this leopard was in deep brush. I reduced my shutter speed, held my breath to steady the camera, and took this photo.

LOISABA CONSERVANCY, KENYA | ISO 3200 | 200MM | 1/500

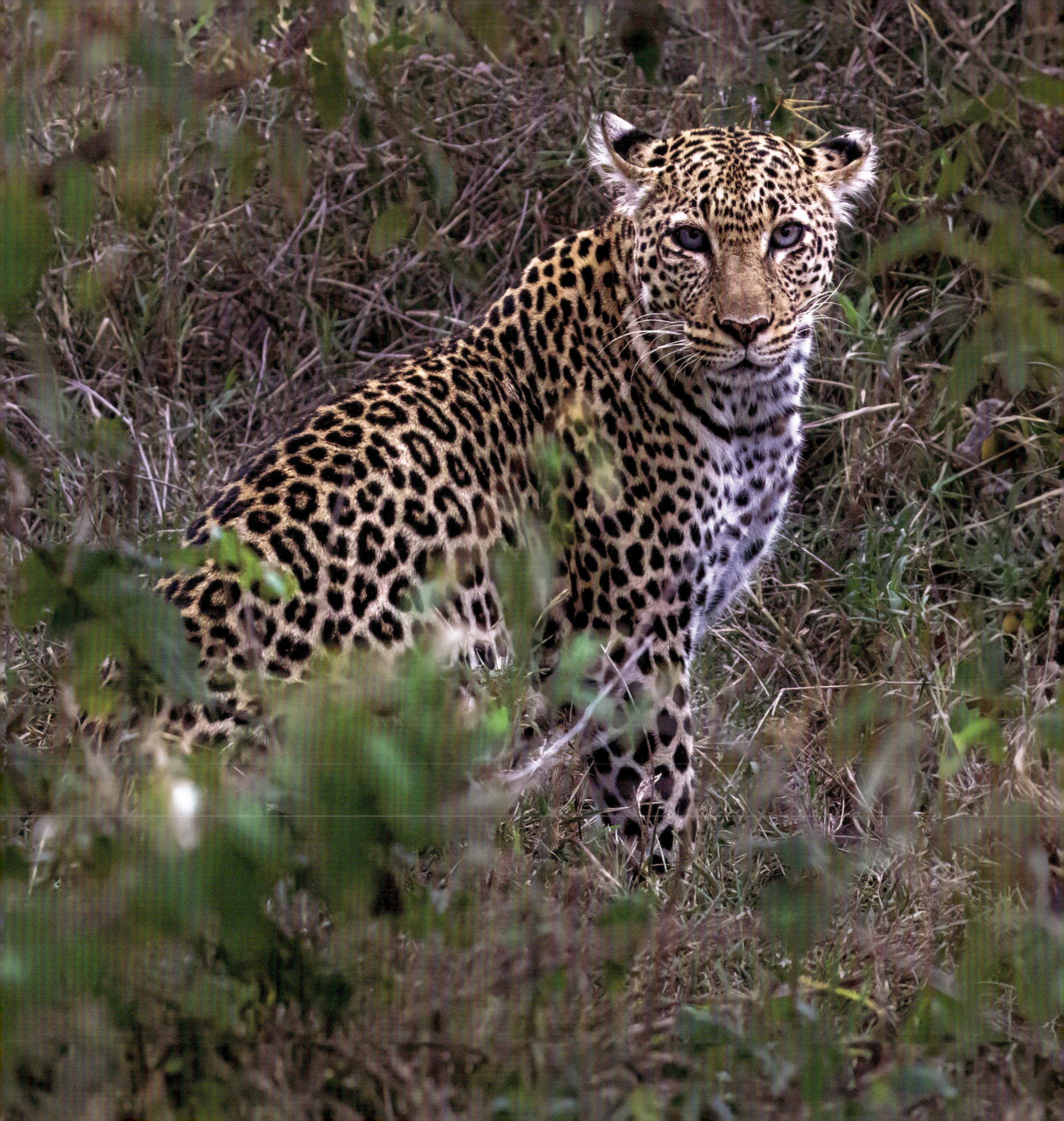

42.

Of Loons and Moons

The common loon probably got its name from its crazy mating rituals and its eerie calls. At dusk, the common loon's enchanting, lyrical calls echo across woods and lakes. It is unforgettable—peaceful, almost mournful, and haunting.

A loon has at least four different calls. When threatened, they give a fluttering call that sounds like crazed laughter. But the one that I most associate with this beautiful bird is the double-noted wail, which Henry David Thoreau appropriately described as "unearthly."

The "crazy person" connotation of the term "loon" probably comes from a Latin word for the moon, from which we also get "lunar" and "lunacy." In the 1300s, it was widely believed that the moon caused insanity. That's also where the notion of werewolves howling at the moon originated.

This particular loon was not crazy at all. It was demonstrating in eloquent simplicity an important principle of physics, namely the interplay between the surface tension of water molecules and the force of gravity.

The force of gravity elongates the droplet until it overcomes the surface tension holding the droplet together and the drop splits and falls. That is just about to happen here.

Droplet of water off the beak of a loon? What a *crazy* idea.

Photographers always try to capture a unique pose or behavior. In this case, the water droplet seemed to hang forever off the Canadian loon's beak. I was in a boat about 20 feet away. The bird had just surfaced when I snapped this photo.

ONTARIO, CANADA | ISO 1600 | 200MM | 1/2000

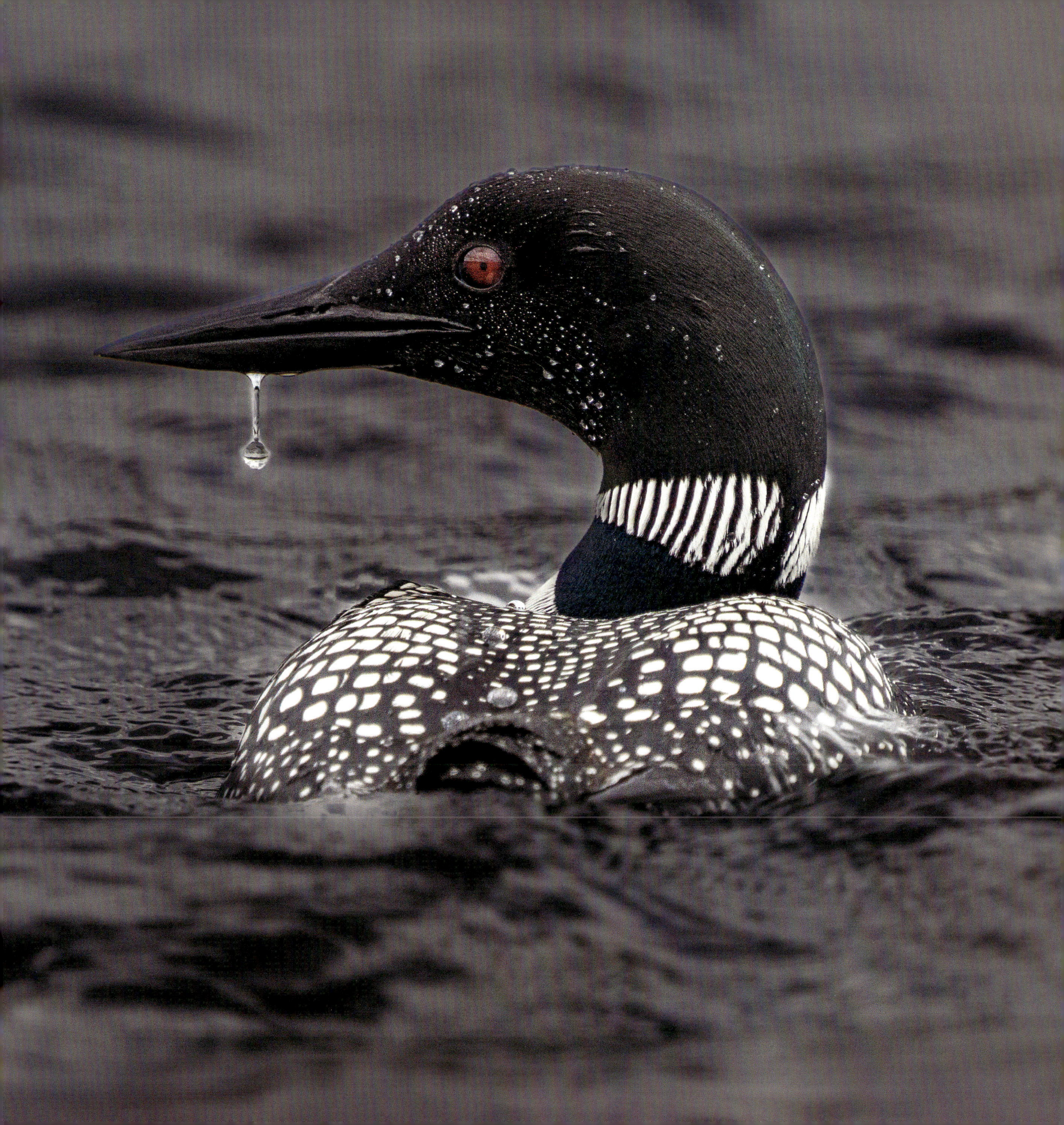

43.

Beauty in the Brambles

In a patch of thornbushes not far from my home, I spotted this swallowtail butterfly flitting from plant to plant. It was incongruous in its surroundings—innocent and lovely, right at home in the midst of brambles and thistles.

Butterflies go from egg to caterpillar to cocoon. At the end of their life, they finally emerge as a flying sprite. But too soon they are gone. For a few weeks in spring, these bushes sport beautiful purple flowers. That is when the butterflies arrive. In a little while, these flowers will wilt and die, leaving only prickly thorns in their place. The butterflies will leave; the beauty will be gone. The thorns will persist.

I grew up when it was still fashionable to be patriotic. My father served in the U.S. Army in the Pacific during most of the Second World War. He loved his country, his family, his God, and his community. My father was unabashedly patriotic because his father was not born in the United States. My grandfather grew up in Greece and faced huge challenges to get to America and build his family's future.

I look forward to the return of America's dream, just as I await the return of the flowers and butterflies each spring, especially when it seems that only the thorns grow. When I hear "America the Beautiful" or "The Star-Spangled Banner" played, or watch fireworks, I still get butterflies. Even when thorns and thistles cover the landscape, America is still beautiful amid brambles.

Butterflies never seem to land. When they do, it may be dark or not well-lit and they will take off quickly. That often makes it hard to get a good exposure. I use the auto ISO feature on my camera to let it make the adjustment for available light automatically.

GARDEN CITY, IDAHO | ISO 1600 | 840MM | 1/1250

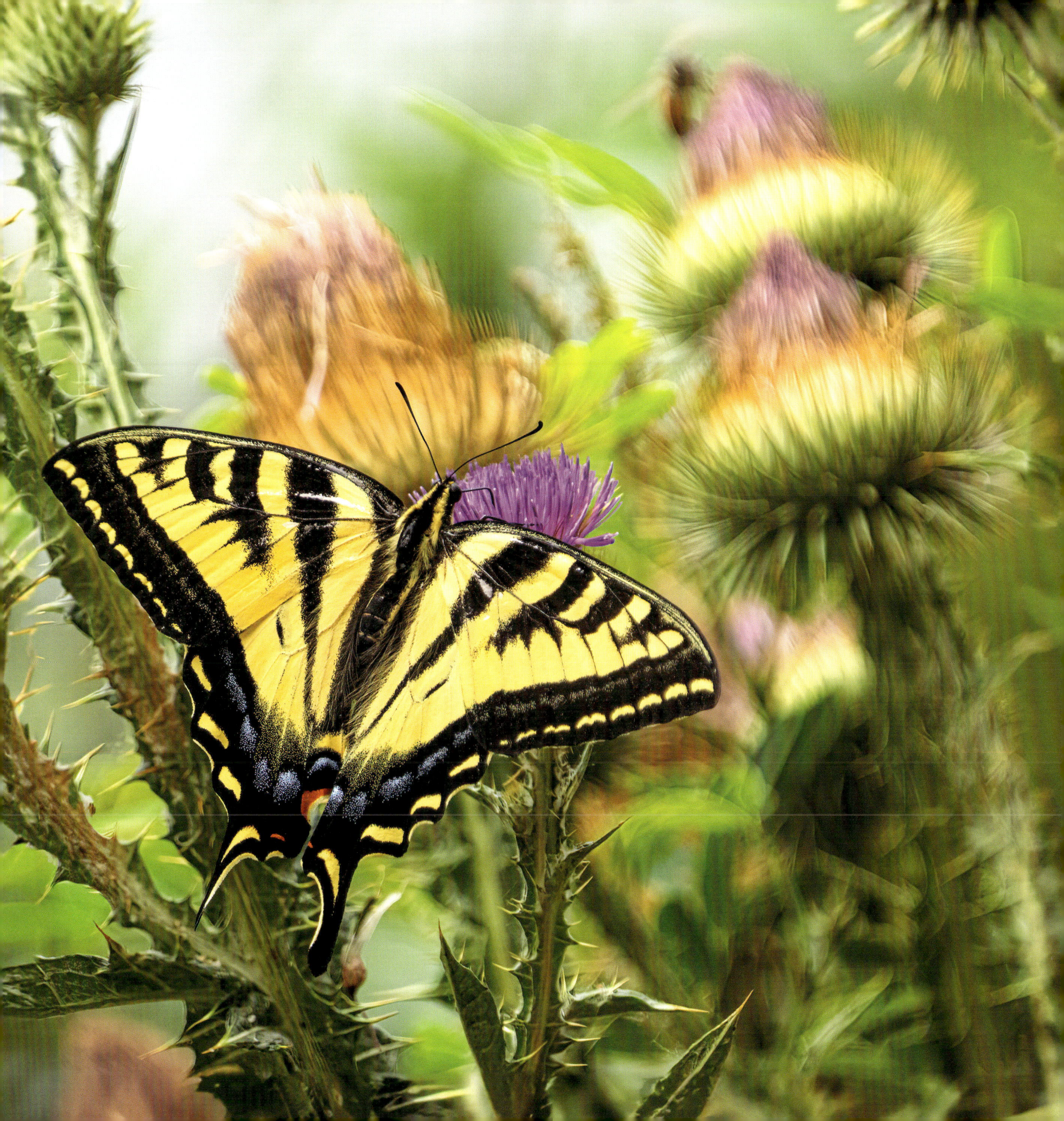

44.

The Road Less Traveled

Every March, up to 60,000 snow geese migrate through Idaho on their way back to their summer breeding grounds in Western Canada and Siberia.

While photographing a huge flock of snow geese ascending in a unified symphony of flight, I noticed a lone bird flying through the center of the flock in the opposite direction. Because I was already focused on the whole flock, the one outlier is out of focus.

Can you relate to that one bird—going against the crowd and flying your own course, or just being out of focus?

Bringing something into focus doesn't change the subject, just its clarity. Focus is entirely dependent upon point of view. In his spot in the sky, that lone goose was in perfect focus. And if my eye had spotted him first, the photo would have proved it, while the rest of the flock would have appeared as a blur. But my attention was drawn first to the crowd. Why? They made more noise. They were more visible. They filled the sky. I almost missed the lone contrarian.

I take comfort in knowing that even if you don't see them or hear about them, there will always be a few free thinkers in the crowd, indifferent to the pressures to conform or compromise, willing to search for the truth. Those who take the road less traveled.

"So Jesus said to the Jews who had believed him, 'If you abide in my word, you are truly my disciples, and you will know the truth, and the truth will set you free.'" John 8:31-32 (ESV)

The flock of snow geese are all in focus. That's because they share the same "plane of focus," which means they are all the same distance from the camera lens.

SNAKE RIVER, IDAHO | ISO 200 | 650MM | 1/1600

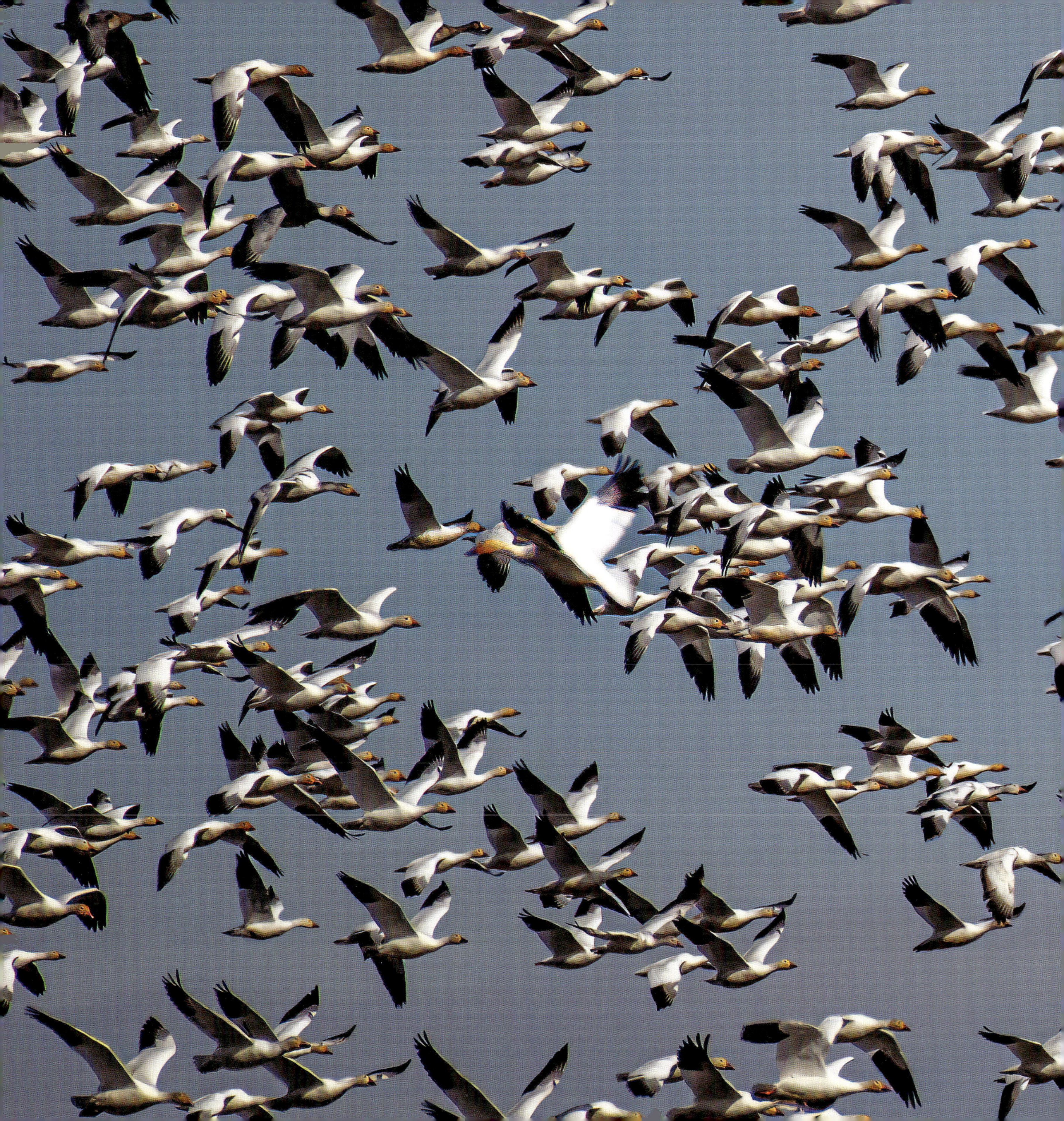

45.

Gobble, Gobble

This big tom turkey struts his plumage in either a show of dominance to another male or to woo a female. While I love turkey almost anytime, Thanksgiving has special memories for me.

On one Thanksgiving, Maureen and I drove with our daughter, Kristen, two hours to my in-laws' house for dinner. On the way, I stopped to meet with Walter and Alice, two clients in their 90s, at their home. We had a new addition to our family, Macintosh, a Scottish terrier puppy who was both adorable and mischievous at 3 months old. Walter invited us to bring the puppy in while we talked. Macintosh sat quietly under their kitchen table. Alice sat in her wheelchair at the opposite end of the table.

While we were talking, Alice dozed off. Then it happened—her mouth fell open and her dentures came loose and dropped to the floor. I immediately looked down to Macintosh, who was eying the object that fell right in front of him. But before Mac could pounce, Walter calmly said, "Why, Alice, you've dropped your teeth again." At which point he scooped them up, wiped them on his shirt, and plopped them back in. Alice never woke up.

In a totally unrelated incident, when we got back in the car, Macintosh jumped in the back. We all thought that was so cute until an odor wafted forward. Our adorable puppy had pooped on the boxes of Marie Callender's apple and pumpkin pies. Being ever so practical, I threw away the boxes but kept the undefiled pies. We were all sworn to secrecy, and we all ate the pies, which were delicious!

I hope your Thanksgiving memories are more savory, but no less sweet.

My go-to aperture for large birds at distance is f/8. "Depth of field" is the width of the area that is in focus. So, if I focus on the nose of the turkey and the depth of field is three feet, his tail feathers will also be in focus.

EAGLE, IDAHO | ISO 1100 | 500MM | 1/1600

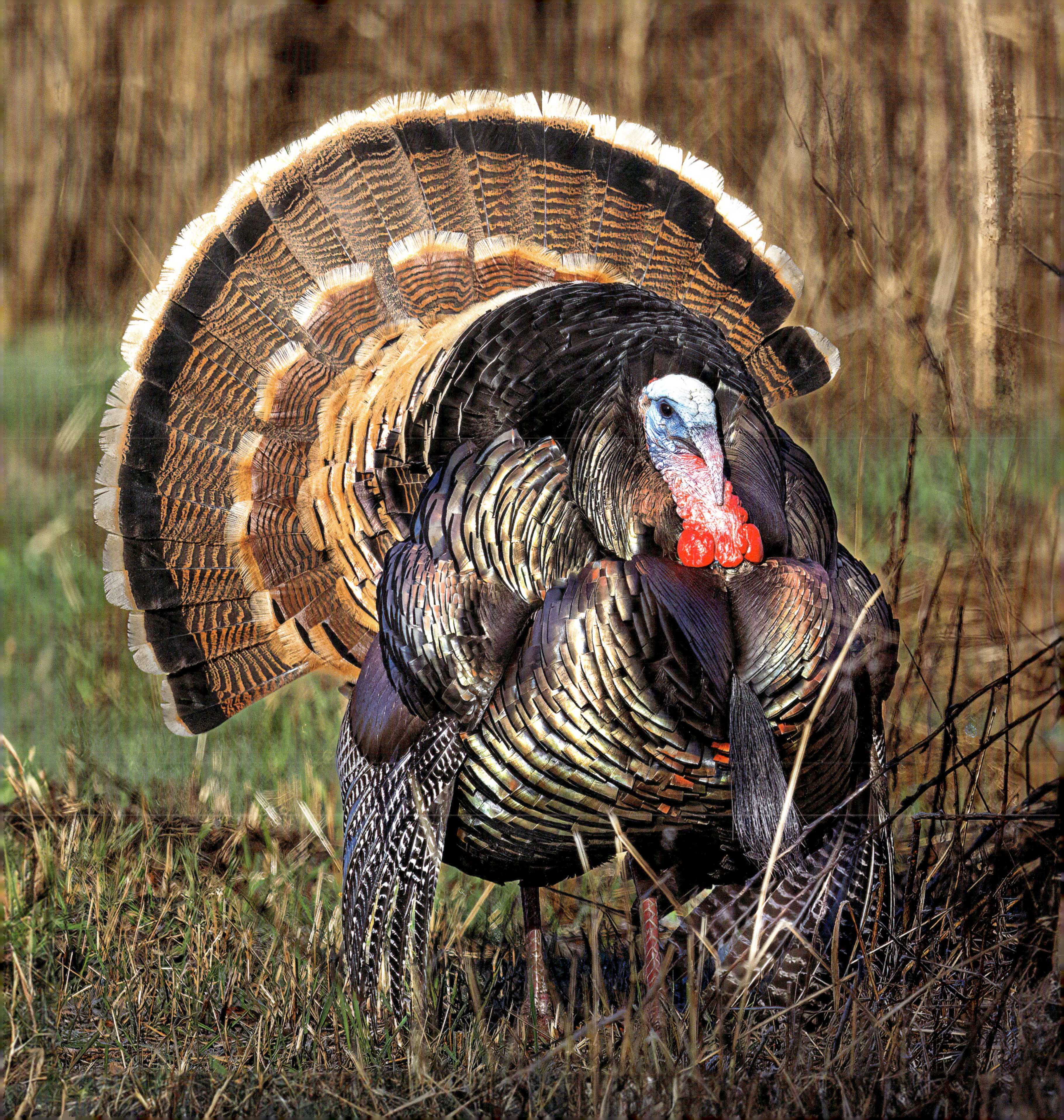

46.

Someone to Watch Over Me

In the still of the night, if you listen carefully, you can sometimes hear the muted hoots of a great horned owl calling to its mate. The owl's call is not the harsh screech of the hawk or shrill cry of eagle or osprey. It is instead warm and inviting, like a welcome caress.

But you rarely catch a glimpse of these all-seeing phantoms in the trees. While I am no longer a child who fears monsters under the bed, I am still not entirely at ease in the dark. I once visited the caverns in Hannibal, Missouri, that inspired Mark Twain's *The Adventures of Tom Sawyer.* While we were underground, the guide had everyone shut off their flashlights. We were instantly submerged in darkness so thick and pervasive that you couldn't see your fingers an inch from your face. I felt utterly helpless and understood for the first time the hopelessness and fear that must accompany physical blindness. Thankfully, he allowed us to switch the lights back on after a few seconds.

You may find the notion of unseen eyes following you in the dark unsettling. I once did. Now, the wise, observant owl is a reminder that we are never out of God's sight. Jesus told his disciples, "Are not two sparrows sold for a penny? Yet not one of them will fall to the ground outside your Father's care. And even the very hairs of your head are all numbered. So don't be afraid; you are worth more than many sparrows." (Matthew 10:29-31 NIV)

We need light to see in the dark. Our eyes can't create light or see anything without it. Even the owl, which can see in extremely dim light, still needs some external light in order to see at all. But God's vision pierces any darkness. After all, he is the author of light.

Owls are most active in the evening or early morning when light is scarce. To illuminate this owl, I overexposed the sky behind it. I set my camera's meter for center-weighted metering, exposing for the bird and not the entire scene.

BOISE RIVER GREENBELT, IDAHO | ISO 1600 | 606MM | 1/1000

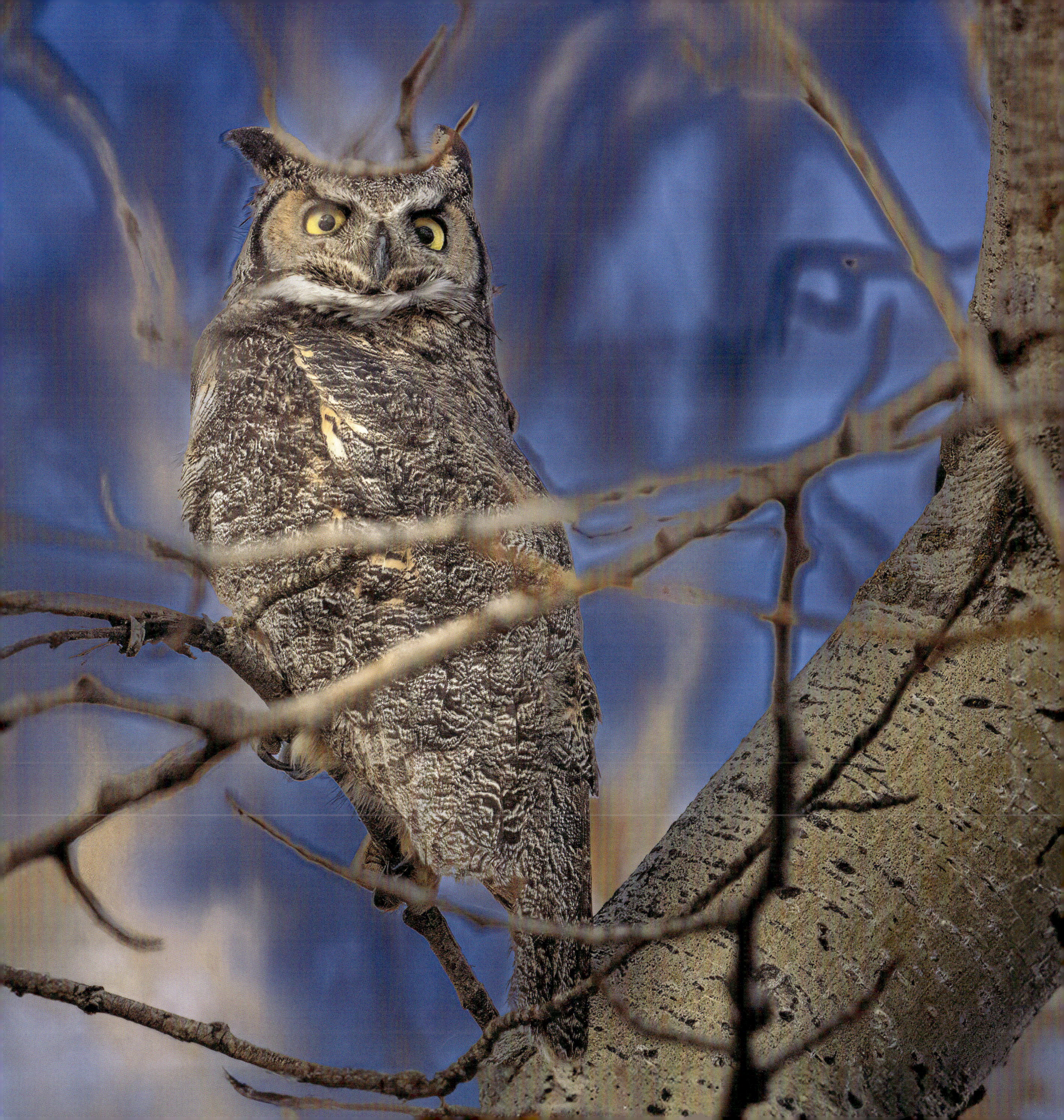

47.

The Maltese Falcon

The American kestrel, nicknamed "the Mighty Little Killer," is North America's smallest falcon. At nine inches long and less than five ounces, it is about the weight of an average smartphone. But this little bird is fearless. The kestrel swoops down from a high perch or from mid-air to snatch everything from flying insects to squirrels or small birds. It is so agile and has such blazing speed that it often catches birds, bats, or insects in flight. While no match for a peregrine falcon's speeds of up to 240 miles per hour, the kestrel's speed still clocks a respectable 60-70 miles per hour in a dive.

One of my favorite films is *The Maltese Falcon*, a murder mystery in 1940s San Francisco involving a quest to retrieve a priceless statue of a black falcon, encrusted with precious gems beneath its black onyx surface. The hero of the story is private eye Samuel Spade, played brilliantly by Humphrey Bogart.

Perhaps because Sam Spade is supremely confident regardless of the odds against him, or perhaps because he is cool, shadowy, and dark, these little mighty killers remind me of him.

This small bird fights well above its weight class, is utterly fearless, resourceful, relentless, and deadly. Hawks or eagles will give up on prey that manages to hide out of sight; the kestrel will dive right into a thicket after a small animal on the ground. On a hunt, the kestrel rarely gives up the chase.

This tiny raptor is the classic little guy we love to root for. As they say, "It's not the size of the dog in the fight; it's the size of the fight in the dog."

After taking this photo, I missed a far better shot. Seconds after I put my camera down, a second kestrel attacked this one and tried to steal the mouse. Lesson learned.

EAGLE, IDAHO | ISO 1250 | 840MM | 1/3200

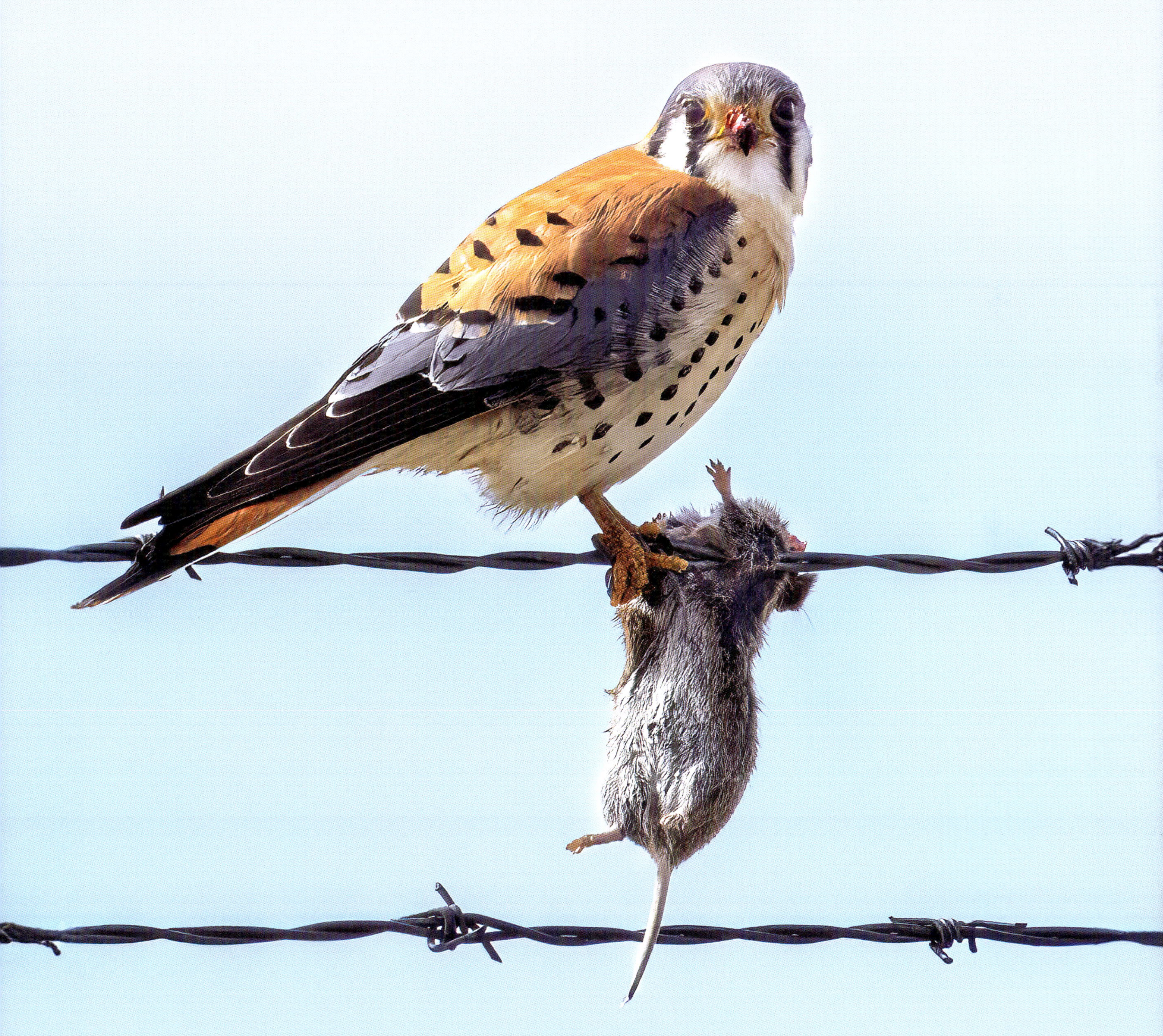

48.

Strike Up the Band!

With its chest out and wings outstretched, this great blue heron reminds me of Robert Preston in *The Music Man*, leading a high school band in a parade down Main Street. While often ungainly and awkward in appearance, when a three-foot-tall Heron strikes a classic pose like this one, it is as graceful as a ballet dancer, presenting itself with poise and aplomb.

The great blue heron is a classic. The ancient Greeks believed it was a messenger from the gods, sent by Athena or Aphrodite, goddesses of wisdom and love. The Celts also revered herons in this way.

To Native Americans, the heron symbolizes wisdom and good judgment. One of their myths holds that the hummingbird challenged the heron to a race to claim all the fish in the lakes and rivers. The heron flew slowly as the hummingbird zipped far ahead; but the heron never stopped, while the hummingbird slept at night. The result was that the heron won the race and now gets to eat fish, while the hummingbird must live on insects and nectar from flowers.

You can learn valuable lessons from the heron. I have watched one crouch silent and still on a river bank for what seemed like an eternity before suddenly jabbing its beak into the water to snatch a fish. The great blue heron is the epitome of concentration and patience—never in a hurry, but always well-fed.

Aesop, the ancient Greek writer of fables, coined the axiom "slow and steady wins the race." Consistency is better than haste. You often get better results by taking the time to do it right.

This heron had just landed in the shallows in Puget Sound where I was photographing eagles, and it caught my eye. It was a lucky shot, but it does seem that the more shots you take, the luckier you get.

PUGET SOUND, WASHINGTON | ISO 800 | 500MM | 1/2500

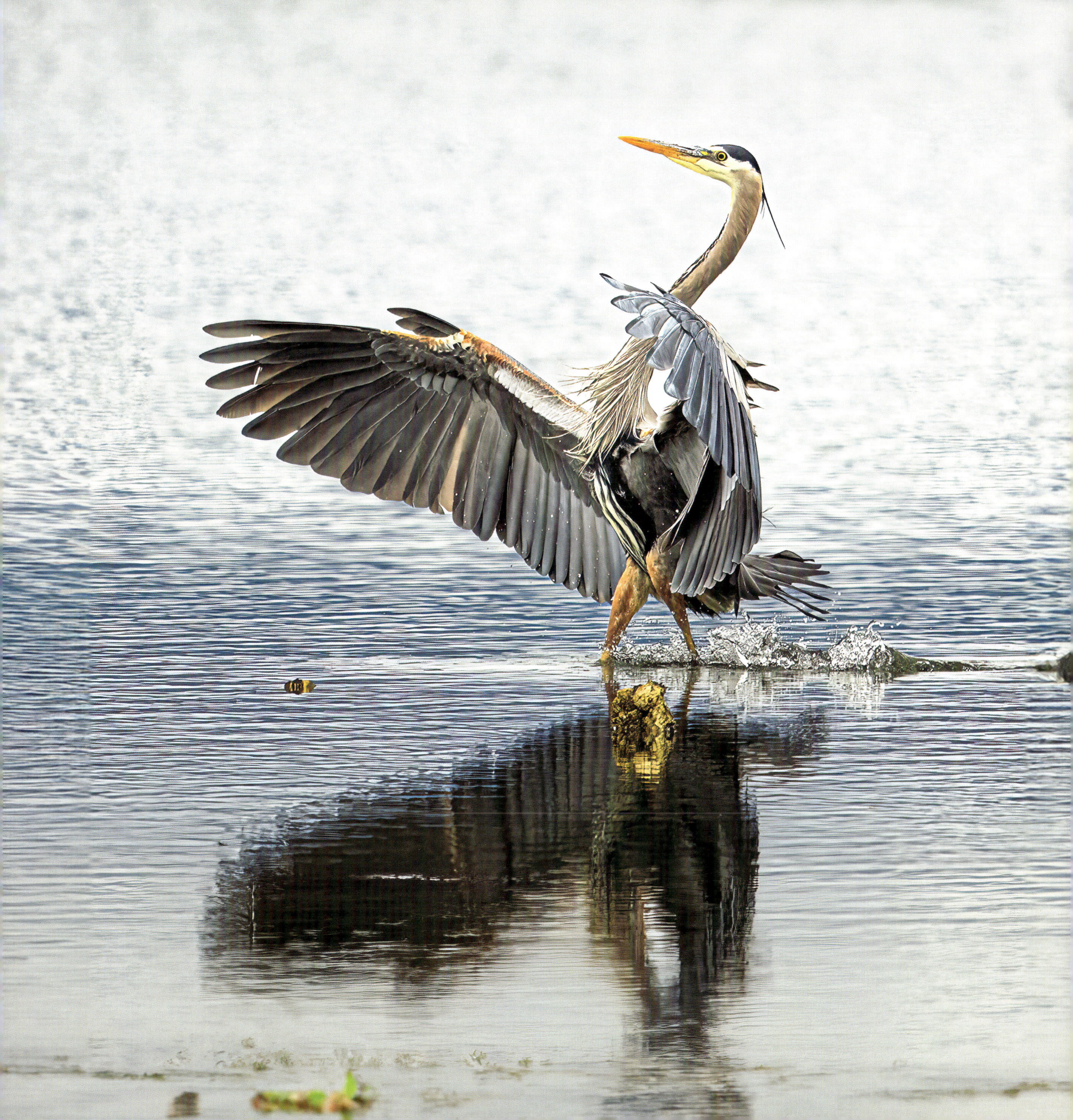

49.

The Heart of the Matter

This little elephant has found the ideal spot to bask in the safety of its mother's love.

Scientists have long known that elephants are capable of complex thoughts and emotions. The playfulness and joy that a mother elephant expresses around her baby is both palpable and poignant. This calf is no longer tiny, but still small enough to walk underneath his mother. But even when a calf is newborn, the mother never steps on it. At all times, she is in constant contact, lifting and carrying it with her trunk. She shelters her calf from lions and other predators, as well as the hot African sun. When the herd is on the move, her calf keeps close by holding her tail in its trunk. A mother elephant's bond with her calf lasts for a lifetime, which may be 50 years or more.

Greek philosophers believed that the heart was the seat of all emotions, including love. The love that a mother elephant has for her baby is evident in how fiercely she defends her offspring and how long they stay closely connected. After almost two years in its mother's womb, a baby elephant will remain inseparable from its mother for its first five years. It seems fitting that a mother elephant's heart matches its love. A mother elephant's heart composes about 0.5 percent of her body weight, averaging between 26.5 and 46 pounds. But it seems much bigger than that in real life.

The human mind interprets images on a horizontal plane as feeling stable, while images on a vertical plane are seen as powerful. Here, that combination is illustrated.

AMBOSELI NP, KENYA | ISO 1600 | 600MM | 1/1000

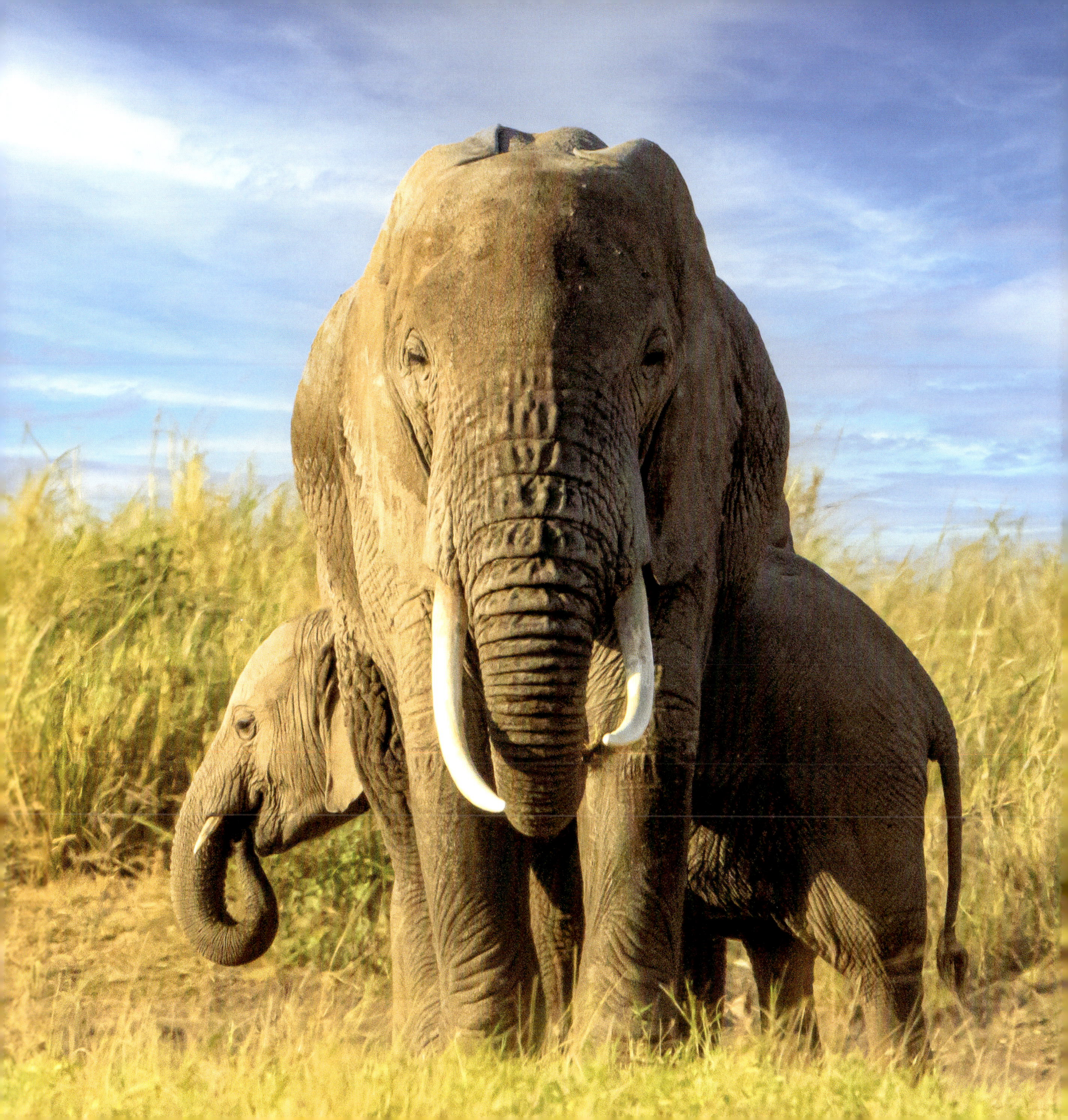

50.

The Saddle Shoe Duck

This is a male northern shoveler, one of 23 species of ducks that winter in Idaho. I call them the "saddle shoe" duck because they have a green saddle over a white chest with a rust-colored underbelly. The name "shoveler" refers to their shoehorn-shaped bill used to strain microorganisms from mud on pond and river bottoms.

When I was growing up, saddle shoes were the rage in school. But my parents didn't have the extra money to satisfy my craving for cool footwear. As an adult, I sprung for a pair of brown and white saddle shoes to play golf. I still have them and still think they are cool. Call me old-fashioned.

For those of you who are more familiar with Air Jordans, a saddle shoe is a low-heeled oxford in white leather. The saddle is a contrast-colored leather piece stitched across the shoe's instep. While the saddle is usually in black, my favorite color is green and that's the shoe I wanted when I was in grade school.

In the 1920s, the popularity of saddle shoes exploded alongside the creation of the jitterbug and Lindy hop dances, and in the 1950s, no poodle-skirted bobby-soxer left home without that essential fashion accessory.

Northern shovelers will raise their young here in Idaho but leave us to summer in Canada. But never fear—just like an old-fashioned accessory that always comes back in style, the northern shoveler will return next spring. After all, it is a very comfortable duck, just like a good pair of saddle shoes.

Capturing a bird in flight requires skill. My typical settings are 1/2000 shutter speed, f/6.3, and a varied ISO depending on available light. For smaller birds, the shutter speed is 1/3200, and for larger birds, the aperture increases to f/8.

EAGLE, IDAHO | ISO 1600 | 840MM | 1/3200

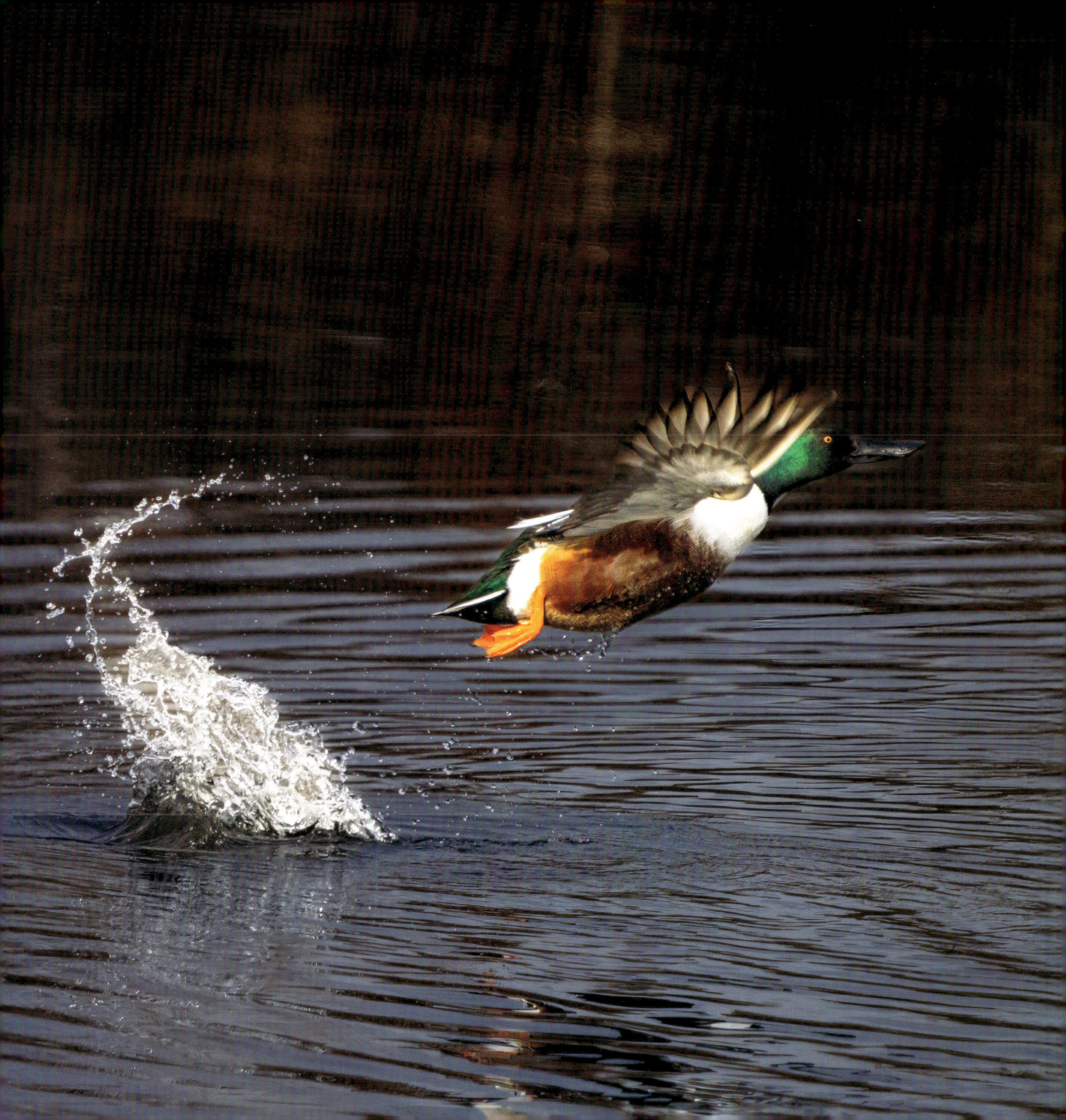

51.

The Wings of Eagles

Birds, like humans, have emotions and feelings. Eagles mate for life and are tender and attentive to their young. Just like us, when a member of their family dies, the survivors grieve the loss.

For the last four years, a pair of eagles have returned each December to the same nest on the Boise River. One May, they lost their only eaglet in an untimely snowstorm. Within days, they abandoned the nest and left the river and I feared that they would never return. The following December, to my delight, the eagles came back. I saw them perched within a hundred yards of their nesting tree. Only time will tell if they reclaim their old nest.

Life and hope endure, even after grievous loss. To me, the eagles' homecoming illustrates hope, renewal, and the resilience of the spirit. The eagle was chosen as our national symbol because of its strength and tenacity. That's also why it was the banner emblem of Rome's armies. But the softer traits of this noble bird are just as worthy. Eagles are loving parents and mates. In fact, the Bible uses this fact to describe God's enduring love.

"He found him in a desert land, and in the howling waste of the wilderness; he encircled him, he cared for him, he kept him as the apple of his eye. Like an eagle that stirs up its nest, that flutters over its young, spreading out its wings, catching them, bearing them on its pinions, the Lord alone guided him . . ." Deuteronomy 32:10-12 (ESV)

Whatever trials come your way, remember that God loves you like the eagle.

This pair of eagles illustrates the power of diagonal lines to create dynamic tension and body position to create balance in the composition. The one on the left faces right and the one on the right faces left.

EAGLE, IDAHO | ISO 800 | 840MM | 1/2500

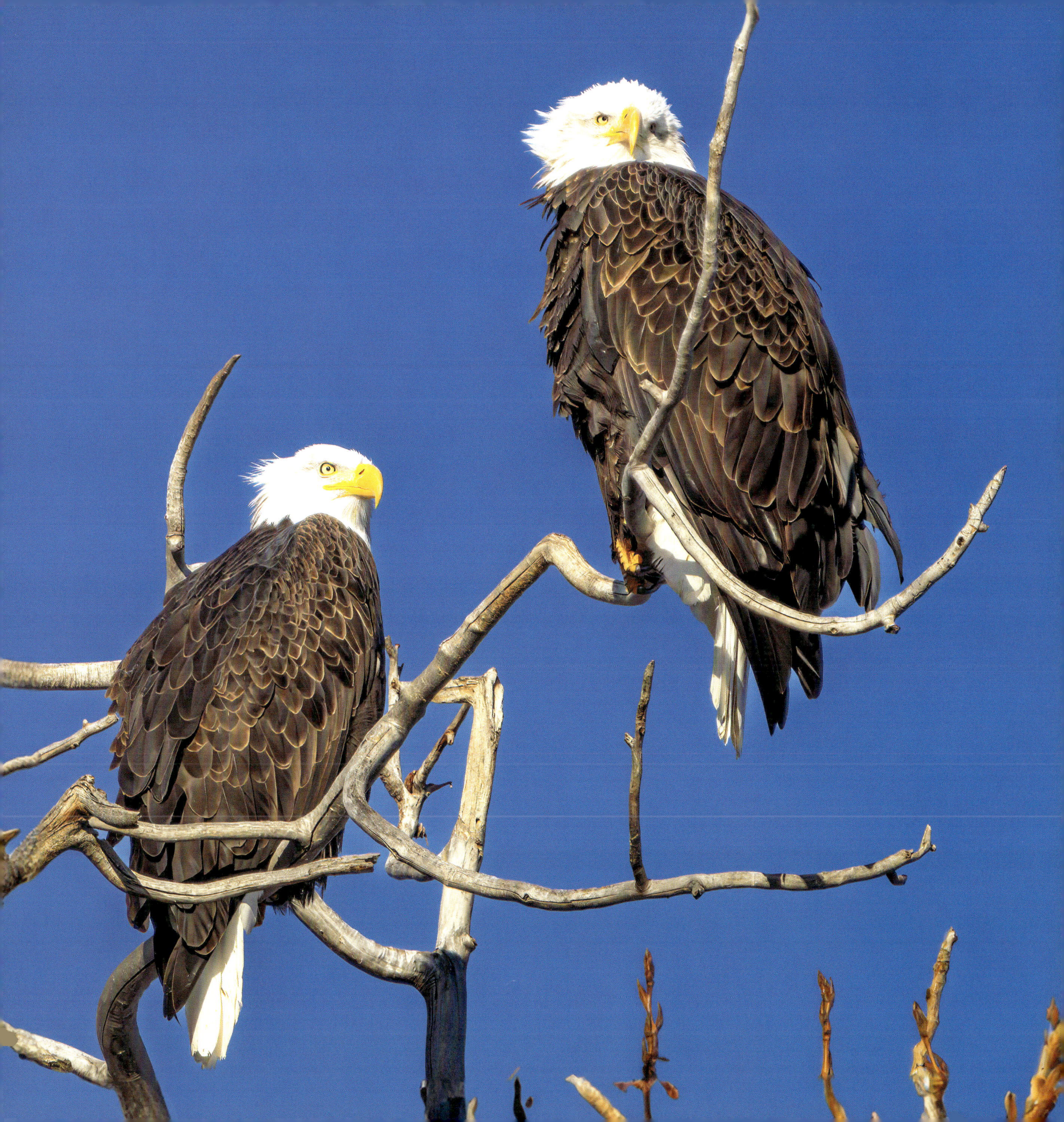

52.

Time Marches On

Over four million wildebeest migrate clockwise in an oval pattern from northern Kenya to the Serengeti in Tanzania every spring and continue back north across the Masai Mara the following fall. They are accompanied by approximately 600,000 zebras and 400,000 antelope.

Their crossing of the Mara River is one of the greatest spectacles of the natural world and is awe-inspiring. It's overwhelming to watch thousands of wildebeest pressing toward and leaping from the banks of a crocodile-infested river and being surrounded by a stampede of animals that make the ground thunder with a noise so loud you can't hear or speak.

Wildebeest are constantly moving from birth to death. Our lives aren't much different. The Greek philosopher Heraclitus remarked that the only constant in life is change. He compared the passing of life to the flow of a river and said you could never step in the same river twice.

Jesus's brother, James, told us, "Yet you do not know what your life will be like tomorrow. For you are just a vapor that appears for a little while, and then vanishes away." James 4:14 (NASB)

Time passes; seasons come and go; we age. Psalm 90:12 (NIV) tells us, "Teach us to number our days, that we may gain a heart of wisdom."

As I grow older, I have come to accept the passage of time with grace. While I will always treasure the memories of past seasons and loved ones now departed, I won't live in them. Instead, I will welcome each new season, knowing it is one more opportunity to make new memories with the people I love.

Photographing the wildebeest migration was a challenge because there was action everywhere. It was easy to just "spray and pray," hoping to get some good shots. I resisted the urge and looked for individuals with a story to tell.

MARA RIVER, KENYA | ISO 1600 | 600MM | 1/3200

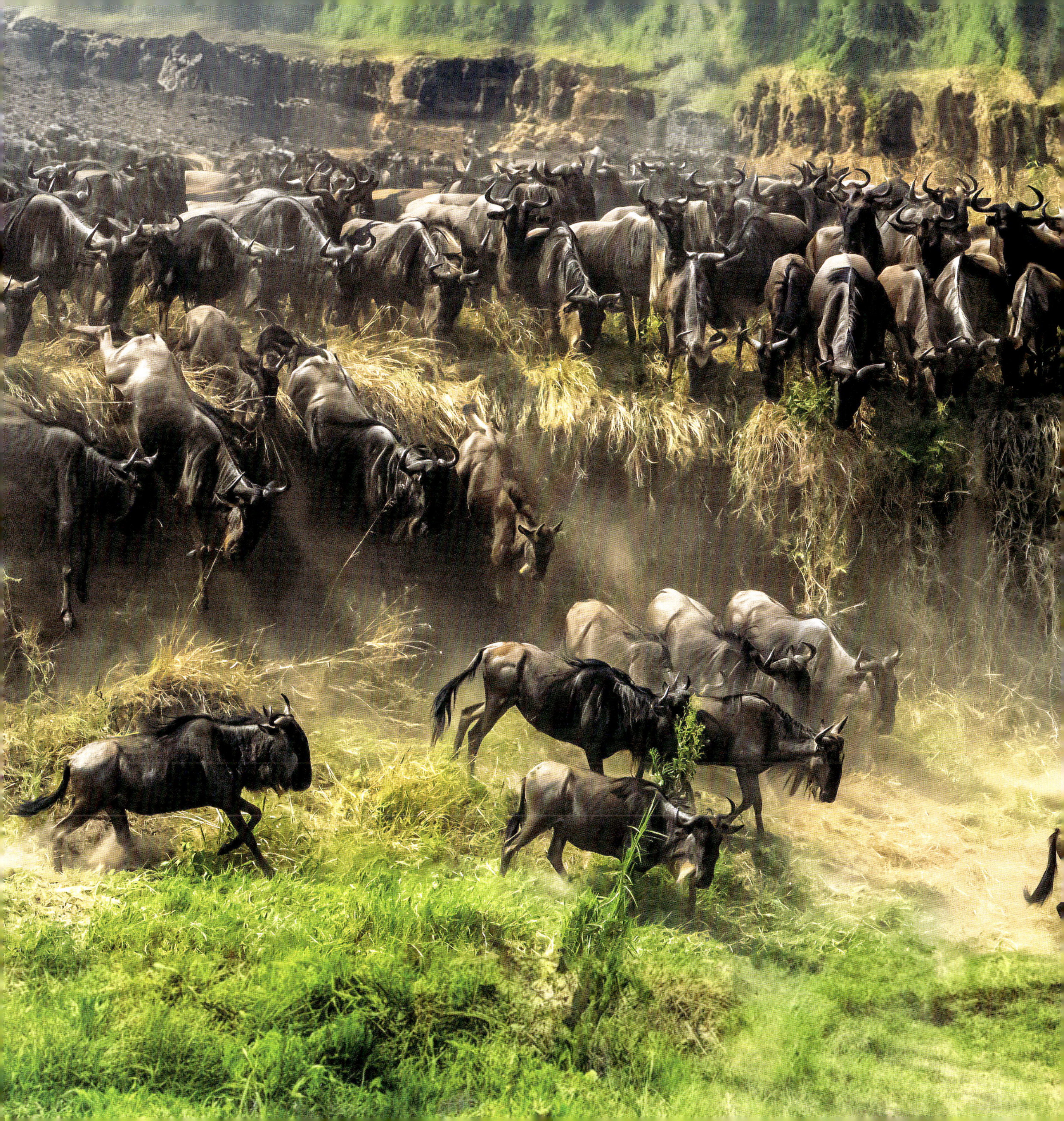

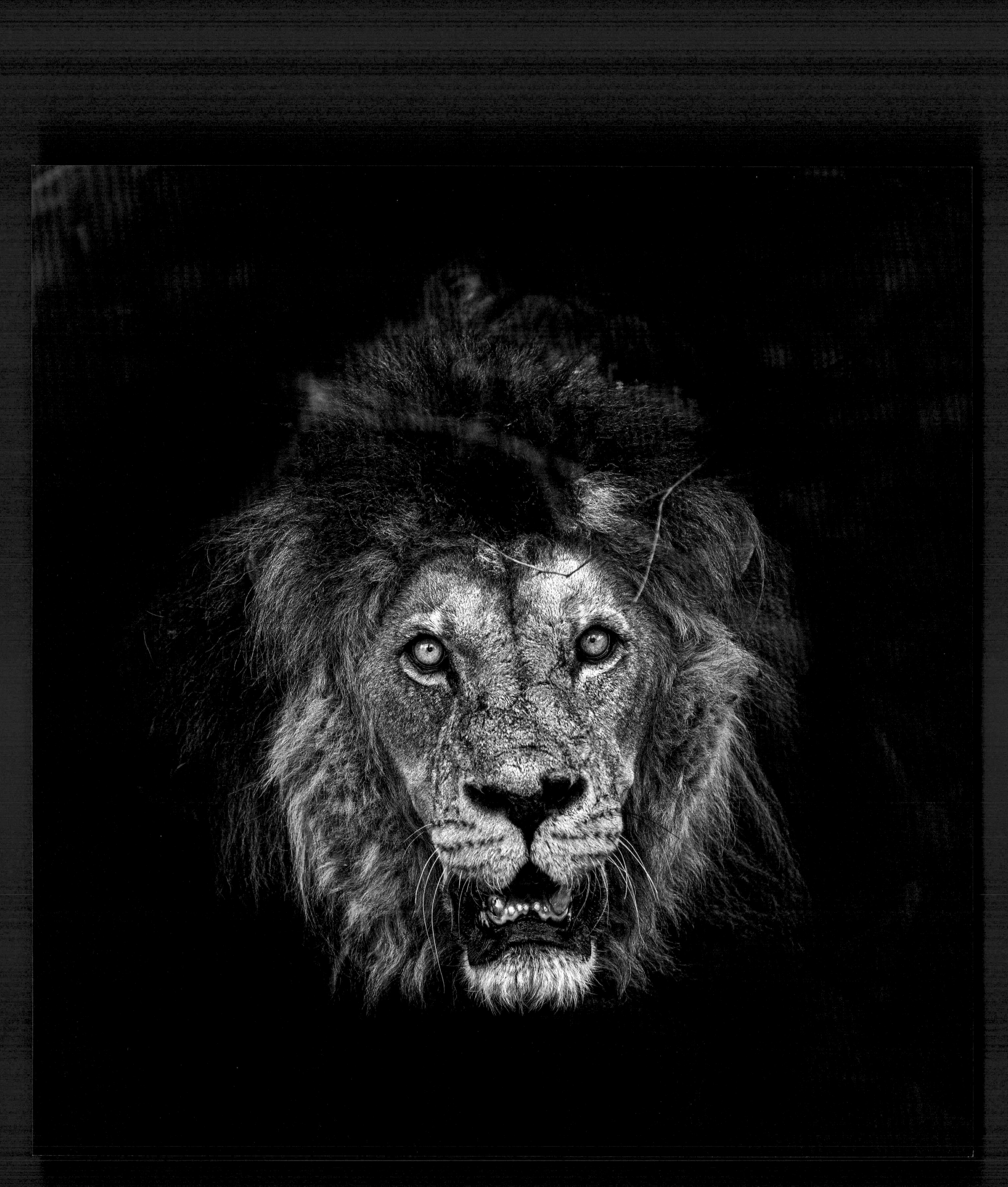

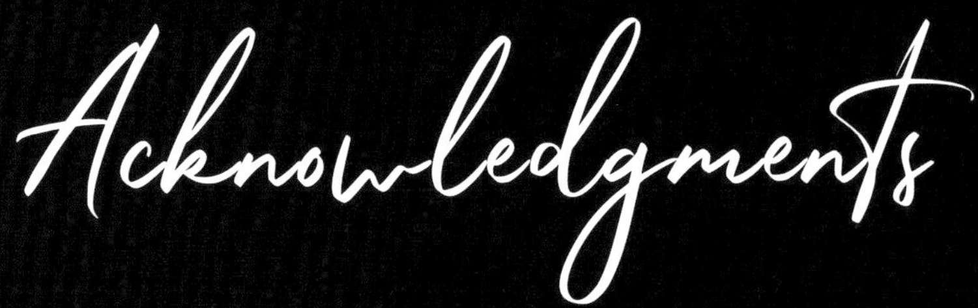

"The Lions"

Ada County Parks and Waterways
Boise Parks and Recreation
Eagle Parks, Pathways and Recreation

I acquired my love for photography, and in particular wildlife photography, on the Boise River Greenbelt on the banks of the Boise River. I watched eagles, ospreys, great horned owls, kestrels, red-tailed hawks, great blue herons, and 20 varieties of migrating ducks, as well as woodpeckers and flickers, right at my back door.

We are blessed with a richly preserved greenbelt, carefully tended and welcome to wildlife, thanks in large part to the great work of our parks departments in Ada County, Boise, and Eagle. I am particularly blessed to have friends like Bill Benko, Cindy Busche, and Tom Harshfield, some of the wonderful caretakers of our Boise Greenbelt.

I consider them "my lions" and deeply appreciate their good work.

Further Acknowledgments

Other friends have lent me a helpful hand as well. Joe Efflandt drove his truck over some challenging terrain and hiked with me through sagebrush and brambles to find the wild mustangs. Tom Goettsche spent countless hours solving the mysteries of Adobe Lightroom for me, as well as spending time in the field. And Lou Esposito trekked with me on more than one occasion in search of eagles, owls, and elk.

Thank you to the Aloha Publishing team for bringing this to life. The ultimate thank-you is to my wonderful wife, Maureen. Without her constant encouragement, support, grace, and love, this book would never have become a reality. I love you.

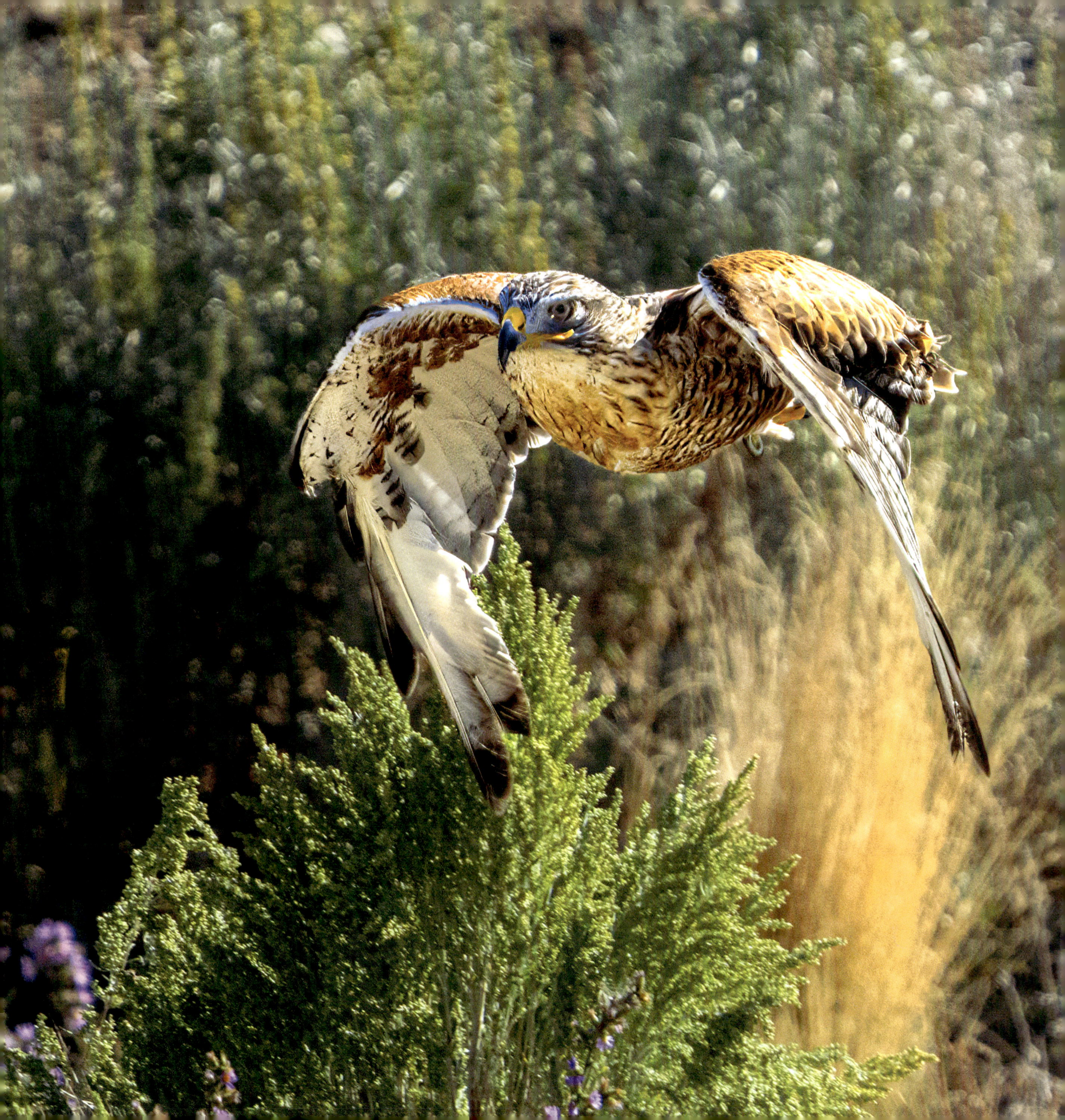

Engage

This magnificent bird of prey is the ferruginous hawk, largest of the soaring buteo hawks. As you can see in this photo, it holds its wings in a shallow V while soaring, before swooping down to catch rabbits, squirrels, or other prey. It is a "threatened" species of raptor, with fewer than 4,000 pairs worldwide and in decline. Over half of all species of raptors are threatened and in serious decline worldwide.

The Peregrine Fund has worked over the past 50 years to conserve peregrine falcons, California condors, and hundreds of other species of birds of prey.

The theme of this book is "reflections," inspired by engagement with wildlife.

If any of the photos or stories in this book have touched your heart, you might consider supporting the essential work of The Peregrine Fund. They have brought back the California condor and many other species from the brink. We still have time to prevent the extinction of our other magnificent raptors.

If you would like a presentation by this author or to purchase this book in quantities of 10 or more, please send an email to AlohaPublishing@gmail.com or visit ChristTroupis.com.

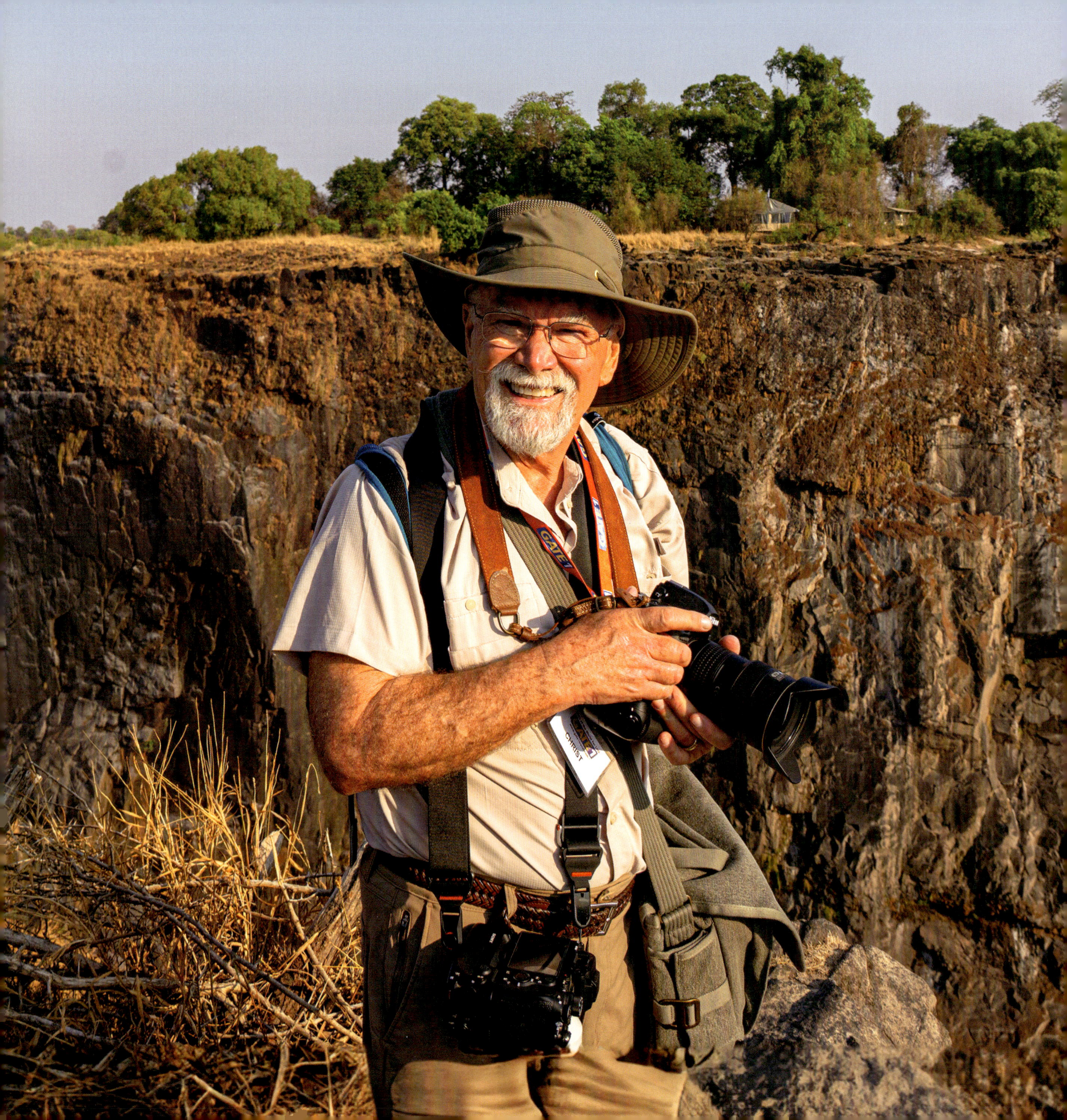

About the Author & Photographer

The stories we hear and those we tell connect, educate, entertain, and inspire us. Christ Troupis is a storyteller. It is something he learned listening to his Irish mother and grandmother, both avid storytellers. In 40 years of practice as a trial lawyer, Christ used stories to keep the jury's attention, persuade, and reduce complex cases to simple principles.

When he retired in 2016, Christ decided to pick up a camera and pursue a new obsess . . . er, passion—capturing the beauty of God's creation while spending time in the peaceful stillness of nature. Soon, his love for storytelling and wildlife photography blended; Christ started sending out emails of photos and the stories they inspired to friends, family, and folks he met on the Boise River Greenbelt.

Christ selected the smiling giraffe for the cover of this book because it befits his personality. Christ is known for his infectious laugh, engaging smile, and gentle spirit. He chose the pair of eagles for the back cover because they represent his hopes and aspirations. God's presence has been his paramount influence throughout his life. Not surprisingly, one of his favorite Bible verses is Isaiah 40:31 (NLT):

> *But those who trust in the Lord will find new strength.*
> *They will soar high on wings like eagles.*
> *They will run and not grow weary.*
> *They will walk and not faint.*

Christ and Maureen Troupis have been married for more than 37 wonderful years. After raising their daughter, Kristen, Maureen joined Christ as the manager of his law office. They are best friends and spend nearly every minute together, in work and play. Together, they continue to experience the beauty of nature, love of God and family, and the fellowship of good friends.

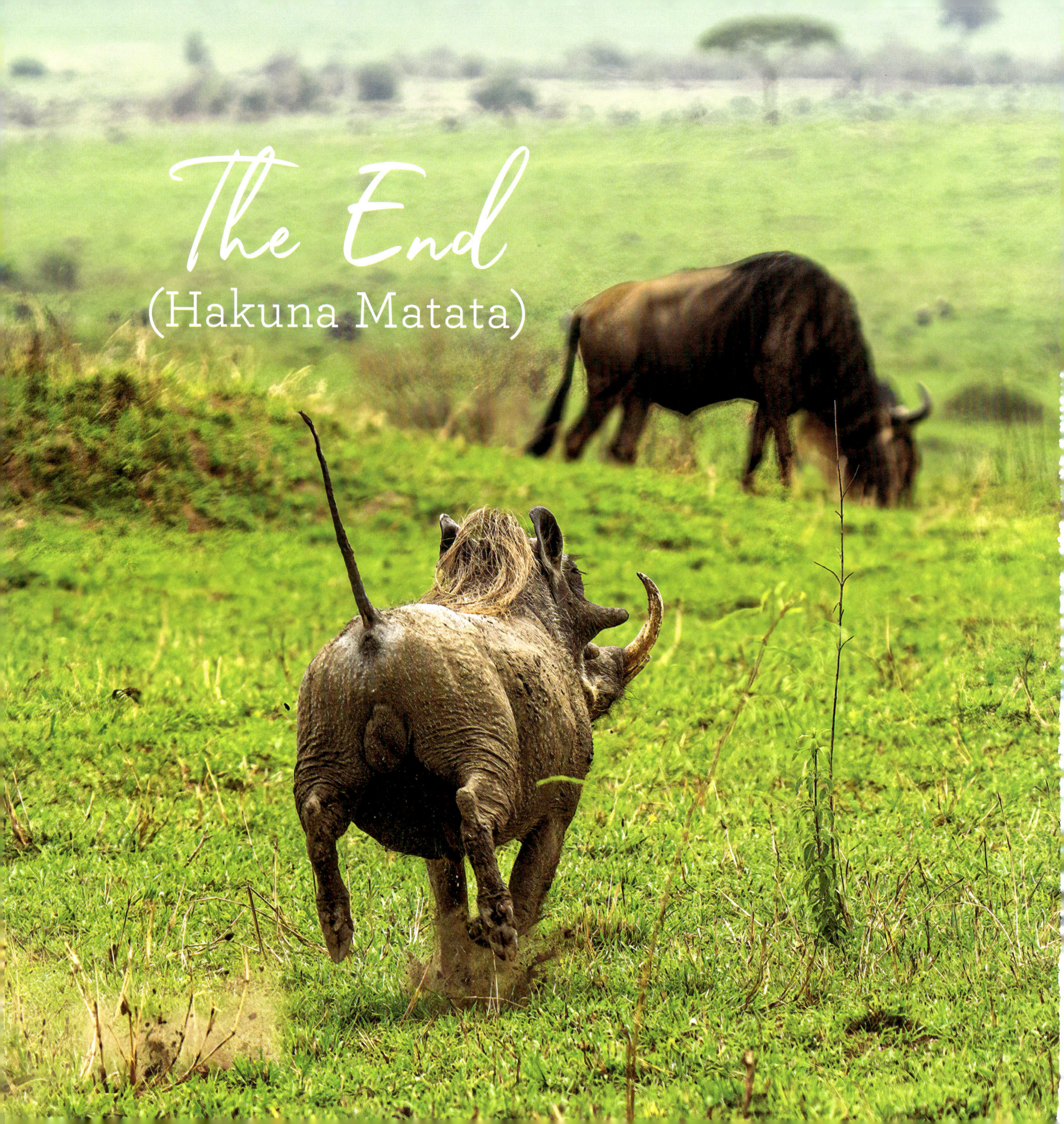

The End
(Hakuna Matata)